GALVANIZED VIRGINIANS

IN THE

INDIAN WARS

HISTORY BOOKS BY THE AUTHOR

The Story the Soldiers Wouldn't Tell

The Attack on Taranto

Tarnished Eagles

Civil War Bawdy Houses

Lincoln and Military Justice

Tarnished Scalpels (with Jack Welsh)

Swamp Doctor

VD and the Lewis & Clark Expedition

Confederate Heroines

Sexual Misbehavior in the Civil War

Mystery of the Bones (with P Willey)

Andersonville to Tahiti

Chinese Soldier in the Indian Wars

Confederate Death Sentences (with Lewis Laska)

Love & Lust: Intimate Civil War Letters

Merciful Lincoln

Utterly Useless Union Officers

Bad Doctors (with Terry Reimer)

Irish & German – Whiskey & Beer

Capital Courtesans

Civil War Rockets

Titanic Madness – Alzheimer's Caused?

Lost Lincolns

Civil War VD Hospitals

Thousand Stories You Don't Know

More Stories You Don't Know

GALVANIZED VIRGINIANS
IN THE
INDIAN WARS

Thomas Power Lowry, M.D.

Idle Winter Press
Portland, Oregon

Idle Winter Press
Portland, Oregon
http://IdleWinter.com

This edition published 2015
Printed in the United States of America
The text of this book is in Alegreya

ISBN-13: 978-0692550748 (Idle Winter Press)
ISBN-10: 0692550747

CONTENTS

ACKNOWLEDGEMENTS

The original list of Confederate soldiers "galvanizing" into the United States Volunteers was created by the late Robert E. Denney. All questions related to Virginia Confederate soldiers were answered by Robert K. Krick. The Rev. Dr. Albert H. Ledoux gave frequent assistance in locating burial sites. Lafcadio Adams gave valuable assistance with graphic matters. Any men tried by general courts-martial were located in the Index Project database, created by Beverly A. Lowry.

PREFACE

Everyone knows what a Civil War battle looked like. While all the original witnesses are gone, we have hundreds of lithographs showing such combat. The lines of men in blue are coherent and close-packed. Before them race the officers, swords held high. They confront an equally organized line of men in butternut or gray, their bayonets, too, flashing in the sun. The Southern officers, with intricate gold arabesques glistening on their sleeves, outshine their Yankee counterparts. One or two fallen men, tucked in a corner of the scene, suggest that battles could be fatal.

Re-enactments attempt to duplicate these scenes but none came close until the filming of *Gettysburg*, in which 15,000 men made manifest the glorious and unforgettable Pickett's charge. A host of men emerged from the woods and marched steadily towards that immortal Clump of Trees a mile away on the horizon. Fifteen thousand bayonets flashed in the sun. Although they faced desperate odds and a veritable hurricane of steel and lead, each Confederate was steadied by the feel of his comrade's shoulders in those close-packed ranks. Beyond his immediate comrades on left and right, were the sight and sound of the other thousands of men. Even when a projectile mowed men down like hay before the farmer's scythe, even when a Minié ball sprayed brains upon the marchers, they went steadily forward, strengthened by their faith in Robert E. Lee, by their noble cause, and by the sheer weight of their numbers. Even in the face of such devastation, the power of close-packed ranks gave them heart and confidence.

Consider now a scene far different from Gettysburg. Pennsylvania was settled, sedate, organized, filled with familiar faces and customs. The great battle was fought in wheat fields and orchards, fought across farms that bore the owner's names, fought by cemeteries where the dead had lain for decades, even centuries.

The new scene also involves Confederates who now wore blue. They were the Galvanized Yankees of the Third Regiment of United States Volunteers, and they were far from any civilization. In fact they were assigned to the middle of the United States, which had no functioning government and no safe transportation. The West Coast was vital, yet isolated. California had gold, essential to funding the Union effort, and two important military installations: Mare

Island Naval Shipyard and Benicia Barracks. Just east was Nevada, whose silver mines also bankrolled the Federal government.

There were no railroads west of the Mississippi River. To send goods, supplies, and men to or from the West Coast there were only two routes. The first was by sea to Panama, across the malaria and yellow fever-filled swamps, and then a second sea voyage. The other route was the Overland Mail Route, a system of horse-drawn stage coaches, dependent on dozens of relay stations. A great rising of the Plains Indians had closed that route, killing travelers, burning the relay stations, and cutting the telegraph wires. The United States was cut in half.

The Department of the Plains was commanded by Gen. Patrick E. Connor, a veteran of frontier warfare. He dispersed the members of the newly arrived 3rd US Volunteers to locations unfamiliar to most Civil War readers: Kearney, Cottonwood, Julesburg, and Laramie. To protect the 600 miles of stage route, the regiment was broken into parties, each with one non-commissioned officer and twelve privates, their camps stationed ten miles apart. One day each party was ordered to march five miles west and return to their camping spot. The next day they marched fives miles east then back to camp. This group of thirteen men, on foot, was supposed to make safe ten miles of road and intimidate the Indians, sometimes described as "the finest light cavalry in the world." In the battles in Virginia, these Southerners were part of the tens of thousands who fought in the Army of

Northern Virginia. Out on the Great Plains, they were lonely, isolated, often outgunned by their opponents, and always outnumbered. A whole new type of courage—the courage of the isolated man—would be required of them.

These Galvanized Yankees were not just a Thin Blue Line, they were a Thin Blue Speck, and yet their record in knitting together a continent is one of courage, endurance, perseverance, and ultimate success. And among those US Volunteers (there were eventually six regiments) were 292 Virginians. The story of these 292 Sons of the Old Dominion have not been fully told before.

They were remarkably loyal to their new allegiance, they earned the respect of the hardened veterans of frontier warfare, and they deserve remembrance. Here is their story.

CHAPTER 1

THE ISSUES

The basic issue facing the armies was a shortage of manpower. Both North and South recruited heavily, using many methods of persuasion—patriotism, local pride, shame, bounties, and conscription—but however fast the bucket filled, it seemed to leak just as fast, through both death and desertion.

How many military and naval men died during the Civil War? Frederick H. Dyer, in his 1908 *A Compendium of the War of the Rebellion*, put the figure for Union dead at 359,528. E. B. Long, in his 1971 *The Civil War Day by Day*, reviewed many sources and concluded that total Federal deaths were 360,222, while the figure for the Confederacy was an estimated 258,000. Alfred J. Bollet, in his 2002 *Civil War Medicine*, gave these figures: Federal deaths 359,528 and Confederate deaths an estimated 200,000. More recent authors have suggested higher figures. While the exact number will never be known, a reasonable estimate would be 600,000 deaths, which includes both North and South, army and navy, disease and wounds.

The other cause of diminishing ranks was desertion. This does not include absence without leave, because an AWOL soldier returns to his unit, sooner or later, usually sooner. The deserter leaves without intention of return. The information on Federal desertion is far more accurate than that for Confederate desertion. Confederate records, which are sadly incomplete, include those tried for desertion, but the numbers who deserted and were never caught are unknown. Consider first, the sources of Federal information.

In March 1863, the US Congress created the Provost Marshal General's Bureau, which collected and published the desertion reports from regimental commanders from March 1863 through December 1865. During this time period, there were 311,267 Union desertions. The Bureau had no data for the period April 1861 through February 1863, so the author derived the number of earlier desertions in the following manner. He and Beverly A. Lowry read all the Union courts-martial for the entire war and, under the aegis of The Index Project, created a Microsoft Access multiple-variable database. Using the desertion figures for March 1863 through December 1865, and the number of desertion courts-martial for that same period, we found that there were 9.6 desertions for every court-martial. (You can't court-martial a man until you catch him.) In the period April 1861 through February 1863, we found 2,684 courts-martial for desertion. Multiplying this figure by 9.6 gave us an estimated 25,765 desertions for the time period before the Bureau began collecting figures. Adding these 25,765 desertions to the Bureau's 311,267 desertions yields a total of 337,032 Union desertions for the entire war. When properly considered this is a shocking figure – twelve percent of the Union army was gone! And never came back. At Gettysburg, the Union forces numbered roughly 90,000. The number of men permanently away from their posts was nearly four times greater than the entire Army of the Potomac in July 1863. There can be no question that the Union had a desertion problem. What about the Confederacy?

In April 1865, as the Union closed in on the Confederate capital of Richmond, the South's leaders decided to burn the tobacco warehouses in that city. Who ordered this disaster—and why—remains a subject of debate 150 years later. One effect was to destroy much of Richmond, including 99 percent of the Confederacy's military justice records. What did survive can be found summarized in two publications: Jack A. Bunch's *Roster of the Courts-Martial in the Confederate States Armies*, and the present author's *Confederate Death Sentences*, co-authored with Lewis Laska. The only extensive record of Confederate courts-martial is the printed General Orders of the Army of Northern Virginia. These roughly 5,000 brief summaries are available on National

Archives microfilm M921, roll 1. They contain 2,274 trials for desertion and 1,302 trials for being absent without leave. There are no records telling us how many men deserted and were never caught, but the anecdotal evidence suggests large numbers.

As the war wore on, the North grew weary. The armies on both sides were fairly well-matched. Their tactics and weapons were almost identical. Their principal leaders were all trained at the same school – West Point. The great and famous battles were mostly meat-grinders with little meaningful change in the strategic picture. The draft was widely unpopular and many men fled to Canada, or California, or went to sea. The Union began two programs for supplementing their forces. One program is well-known; the other has existed in obscurity.

The better-known program was the recruitment, training, and arming of African American men. Beginning in late 1863 and ending in 1866, nearly 180,000 men of color wore Union uniforms. (After the Civil War, black units of so-called Buffalo Soldiers fought in the Indian Wars.)

Less well-known was the recruitment of Confederate soldiers being held in Union prisoner of war camps. Neither North nor South was prepared to guard, house, and feed large numbers of prisoners, and the privations and deaths in those camps have been the subject of many studies. When offered the chance to swear allegiance to the United States, roughly 5,000 Confederate soldiers took that step, put on Union blue, and took up arms, mainly guarding the routes and trails across the western frontier. These units were termed United States Volunteers (not to be confused with other units with "volunteer" in the name) and eventually formed a total of six regiments. The story of these men, and in particular men from Virginia, is the *corpus* of this book.

But before proceeding further we must consider the most common term for these soldiers: "Galvanized Yankees." To keep a steel bucket from rusting it can be coated with zinc, usually by dipping the bucket into a bath of molten zinc. It is still a steel bucket but it has an external coating. By analogy, a Confederate soldier in a Union uniform is still a Confederate, but with an outer coating of Union blue.

CHAPTER 2
THE SOURCES

The beginning point for this essay is the research of Robert E. Denney. Bob, whose remarkable life is detailed in Appendix A, took an interest in "Galvanized Yankees" around 1992 and continued to research them until shortly before his death in 2002. Five days a week, he took the Metro into Washington, DC, and sat at the same table in the National Archives reading room. His self-imposed task was to document every Confederate prisoner of war who took the Oath of Allegiance to the United States and put on the blue uniform of the United States Volunteers.

This involved reading each man's Confederate service record, prison camp record, and US Volunteers record. Many of these records had not been examined since 1865 and were badly faded. The multiple scribes who recorded them were often casual about name spelling. One soldier had his name spelled eleven different ways. These variations called for multiple cross-checking, a task made further difficult by the Southern custom of recording initials instead of spelling out given names. (Think A. P. Hill.) Bob had a master's degree in computer science and created a highly customized version of Microsoft Access. When he stopped work on this project, due to declining health, his database included 3,710 men. Arranged by state, in descending order, he found the following numbers: Tennessee 688; Alabama 564; Georgia 464; North Carolina 421; Mississippi 325; Louisiana 300; Virginia 292; Arkansas 149; Texas 146; Kentucky 132; Missouri 78; Florida 78; and South Carolina 73. The present author does not know if the database covers <u>all</u> of the men who galvanized.

A few months before his death, he handed me a compact disc containing his database and asked that it be made available to the public. He included a few pages describing his research methods, but nothing about how to open the complex web of variables included in the disc. While his verbal instructions were fresh in my mind I printed the column rosters for the fourteen states and a few sample individual reports.

N Last	N First	N MI	CSA_RefRecordName	Expr1004	CSA_Regiment	USA_Rec
Absher	William		William Absher	William	64th Va. Mtd. Inf.	P
Acree	George	C.	George C. Acker	George	19th Va. Cav.	P
Adams	Henry	R.		Henry	37th Va. Inf.	P
Adams	James	M.	James M. Adams	James	38th (Pittsylvania) Va. Inf.	P
Adams	Samuel	H.	Samuel A. Adams	Samuel	28th Va. Inf.	P
Adcock	Roland	T.		Roland	45th Va. Inf.	P
Adkins	Perry	G.		Perry	34th Bn. Va. Cav.	P
Ailstock	Jordan	D.	Jordan Ailstock	Jordan	11th Va. Cav.	P
Akers	Andrew	H.	Anderson ;H. Akers	Andrew	63rd (McMahon's) Va. Inf.	P
Aleshire	David	F.	Frank Ailshire	David	10th Va. Inf.	P
Allen	Perry			Perry	34th Bn. Va. Cav.	P
Alley	Ballard	P.	Richard Allie	Ballard	63rd (McMahon's) Va. Inf.	P
Anderson	Samuel	A.	Samuel Anderson	Samuel	Mosby's Regt. Cav. (Partisan R	P
Anderson	William	H.		William	11th Va. Cav.	P
Andrews	William			William	50th Va. Inf.	P
Arbigast	Ephriam		Ephriam Arbogast	Ephriam	25th (Heck's) Va. Inf.	P
Ayers	Jefferson		Jefferson Aryes	Jefferson	17th Va. Cav.	P
Bailey	Henry			Henry	48th Va. Inf.	P
Bailey	William	L.	William Baily	William	37th Va. Inf.	P
Bain	William			William	13th Va. Cav.	P
Baird	William			William	41st (White's) Bn. Va. Cav.	P
Baker	Noah		Noah Baker	Noah	64th Va. Mtd. Inf.	P
Baumgardn	James	A.	James A. Bumgardner	James	63rd (McMahon's) Va. Inf.	P
Bell	Benjamin	G.		Benjamin	64th Va. Inf.	P
Bell	Charles	A.		Charles	49th Va. Inf.	P
Benson	John	G.		John	25th (Heck's) Va. Inf.	P
Blankenshi	Joseph	T.	J. T. Blankenship	Joseph	25th Bn. Va. Inf.	P
Blevins	Andrew			Andrew	63rd (McMahon's) Va. Inf.	P
Bowles	George	W.		George	30th Bn. Va. S.S.	P
Boyd	Asa	E.		Asa	42nd Va. Inf.	P
Bradley	Phillip		John Bradley	Phillip	24th Va. Cav.	P
Bray	John	T.		John	50th Va. Inf.	P
Bray	Michael	D.	M. D. Bray	Michael	64th Va. Mtd. Inf.	P
Broden	John	W.		John	6th Va. Cav.	P
Brown	Baswell			Baswell	50th Va. Inf.	P
Brown	Horace			Horace	12th Bn. Va. Lt. Arty.	P
Buntrum	William	H.	William H. Brenter	William	42nd Va. Inf.	P
Butler	Andrew	J.		Andrew	41st Va. Inf.	P
Byrd	Thomas	W.	Thomas Bird	Thomas	11th Va. Cav.	P
Caldwell	John	F.	John F. Caldwell	John	5th Va. Inf.	P
Campbell	John	A.	J. A. Campbell	John	31st Va. Inf.	P
Cayson	John	W.	John W. Cason	John	16th Va. Inf.	P
Chaney	William	T.	William P. Chaney	William	22nd Va. Cav. (Bowen's Regt.	P
Cheek	Isaiah		Isaac Check shown in CSA r	Isaiah	50th Va. Inf.	P
Cofer	James	E.		James	42nd Va. Inf.	P
Colley	William		William B. Colley	William	48th Va. Inf.	P
Collins	Daniel	M.	Daniel Collins	Daniel	2nd Va. Inf.	P
Collins	Daniel			Daniel	62nd Va. Mtd. Inf.	P
Collins	John	P	John Collins	John	1st Bn. Va. Inf. (Irish Bn.)	P
Collins	John	W.		John	45th Va. Inf.	P
Collins	Richard	J.		Richard	50th Va. Inf.	P
Colton	William		William Calton	William	48th Va. Inf.	P
Conner	James	A.		James	Capt. Archibald Graham's Co.	P
Cook	Mathew	E.		Mathew	22nd Va. Inf.	P
Cooley	George	W.	George W. Coley	George	37th Va. Inf.	P
Cooper	William			William	47th Va. Inf.	P
Cordill	Abner		Abner Cordell	Abner	63rd (McMahon's) Va. Inf.	P
Cox	Charles	F.		Charles	52nd Va. Inf.	P
Cumby	John		James Cumby, J. J. Cumby,	John	42nd Va. Inf.	P
Cundiff	John	T.		John	55th Va. Inf.	P

Other concerns put the galvanized men on hold for almost a decade. When I returned to the subject, I had forgotten the verbal instructions. Even with help of three computer experts, the disc refused to give up its secrets. Converting it to run on Access 2013 did not help. Thus armed only with the Virginia roster, I had to reconstruct the individual stories of the 292 Virginia galvanized men from other sources. These included civilwardata.com, the National Park Service's Soldiers and Sailors index, and the Compiled Military Service Records (CMSR), held in the National Archives.

A firm called Fold3 has a contract to digitize many types of military records. When the author first began this project, many of the records of the US Volunteers were lost in a bureaucratic limbo twixt paper storage and digital accessibility. But the completion of this process, further aided by colleagues who knew short-cuts in the often arcane Fold3 methods of finding records, has made it possible to read the records of all the galvanized Virginians.

What the present author sought with particular interest was the hardships faced by these men once in Federal service. Anecdotal evidence of their service on the Western frontier suggested frequent death by blizzards, Indian attacks, and malnutrition. A further area of interest was the men's post-war histories. Did they return to their home towns or perhaps go further west, to California and its booming gold economy?

This raises the subject of "regimental histories." Both North and South, regiments were frequently raised in one community and both officers and men were familiar to each other, adding to unit cohesion. When the war was over, the memories of service together were strong. Hundreds of regiments had some member with a literary bent who would compile and publish a history of that unit's suffering and heroic service, often with an annotated roster of all who served. Even today, such histories are still being compiled, usually by the great-grandson of a soldier from that regiment. The classified ads in several current Civil War publications have requests such as this fictitious example: "Seeking letters, diaries, photos, etc. from 35th Delaware Infantry. Contact DelawareBill@gmail.com."

The story is different for Federal regiments, such as US Infantry and US Volunteer regiments. Their troops were drawn from a wide variety of sources and locales. There was little or no community identity, and for the galvanized men, a brass band welcome home was even less likely. "Hurrah for old George, who abandoned our colors and joined the hated Yankees." An oxymoronic cheer indeed. But are there regimental histories of the galvanized men?

There is at least one. History professor Michèle Tucker Butts published *Galvanized Yankees on the Upper Missouri – the Face of Loyalty* in 2003, a work of profound and diligent scholarship. She presents in astonishing detail the triumphs and travails of the First United States Volunteers. As for regiments 2nd through 6th, the current sources are the summaries found in Frederick H. Dyer's magisterial *A Compendium of the War of the Rebellion*, published in 1908 and republished by Broadfoot in 1994. The officers, only one of which had been a Confederate, are covered in *Official Army Register of the Volunteer Force of the United States Army*, published in 1865 by the Secretary of War and republished in 1987 by Olde Soldier Books.

Dorris Alexander "Dee" Brown's *The Galvanized Yankees* (published in 1963) covers all six regiments and is a classic of extensive research and brilliant narrative prose.

There are least two novels about Galvanized Yankees: Troy D. Smith's *The Galvanized Yankees of Company D*, and *Galvanized Yankees*, by Mark Bannerman. They play no part in the current study.

CHAPTER 3
THE MISERS

All Civil War prison camps had one thing in common: hunger. Starvation. Malnutrition. At Andersonville, 13,000 men died. Post-war, Maj. Henry Wirz, Andersonville's commander, was hanged for war crimes. I have read the trial transcript, which contains many letters from Wirz to his superiors, begging for more food, emphasizing that his prisoners were staving to death. Wirz got no help.

His superior, Brig. Gen. John Henry Winder, on June 3, 1864, had been sent to Andersonville to oversee matters there. On July 20, 1864, Winder was appointed to command all Confederate prisons in Alabama and Georgia. Four months later, his duties and powers expanded: he was appointed Commissary of all prisons east of the Mississippi

River. Winder had the authority to make the improvements requested by Wirz. It would seem that Winder was the ultimate authority responsible for the thousands of dead. He escaped post-war punishment by dying February 8, 1865 of a massive heart attack. Had not the Angel of Death visited him as he inspected the Florence Stockade in South Carolina, it might have been Winder, not Wirz, at the end of a rope. However, our study here is of northern prisons and malnutrition on those camps, and before that a digression onto a theme raised by generation of Lost Cause revisionists: "The northern prisons were just as bad as the southern prisons."

An apt commentary upon this issue will be clear to readers literate enough to recall the story of Peter Pan and Tinker Bell. Eric Leonard, Chief of Interpretation and Education at Andersonville National Historic Site, writes: "We have a saying at the park that every time someone utters, 'prisons in the north were just as bad as Andersonville,' a historian loses her wings." The use of death rates creates a sense of false equivalency. Comparing northern prisons with each other and southern prisons with each other can yield some meaningful figures, but north-south comparisons are fraught with cultural and statistical errors. Nevertheless, any reader would wish to see the best estimates currently available and take their meaning with 30 milligrams (one grain) of salt.

As Gen. William T. Sherman's forces approached Atlanta, the Confederate decided to close Andersonville and move its inmates north. Just why seems a mystery. If the men had been left at Andersonville, the Union forces would have had the burden of feeding and caring for them. The prisoners were far too weak to ever again be fighting men. The South could have used the many railroads involved to move their own troops. Did the South fear adverse publicity when the living skeletons would be discovered and exploited by the northern press? What is known is that half the Andersonville men were sent by train, under deplorable conditions, to a new facility at Florence, South Carolina, the so-called Florence Stockade. A very recent study of the Confederate Florence Stockade by the Rev. Dr. A. H. Ledoux, published under the title of *The Florence Stockade: A Chronicle of Prison Life in the Waning Months of the Civil War* gives previously unknown information on that facility. Fr. Ledoux, in a remarkable labor of diligence traced the path and military service records of every man known to been imprisoned at Florence. "Any estimate of the numbers interned at Florence must of necessity be highly tentative. No single list of prisoners exists." The estimates are based on extant exchange rolls and on the estimated number of men on the last two trains to leave Florence. The list also includes the 543 Union soldiers who "galvanized" into Confederate service. (More on them in Appendix B.) Fr. Ledoux's best estimate of the total number of Union men ever interned at Florence is 16,569. The Florence National Cemetery contains 2,746 Union dead, yielding a mortality of 16.57 percent. We will return to the issue of prison mortality after reviewing some of the factors involved.

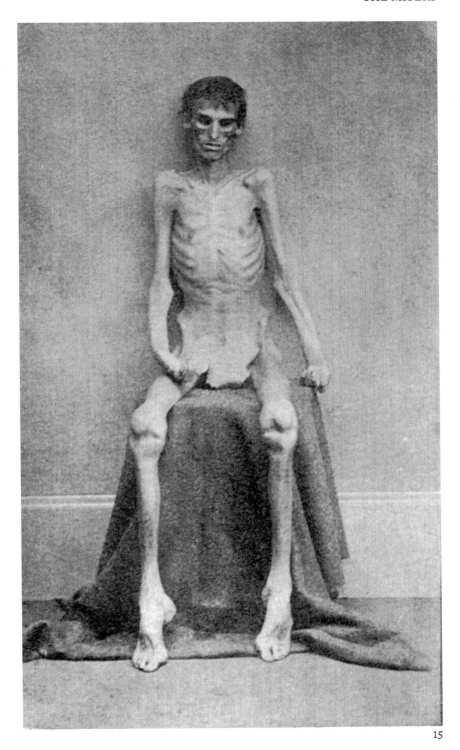

Food in the Northern Prisons

Was there a Union equivalent of the Confederacy's John Henry Winder? There most certainly was an equivalent, a direct equivalent, and his career is well-documented, but before we pass to the man himself we must examine the Old Army, which had rules, regulations, and traditions that, seen in today's light, seem so penurious, narrow-minded, petty, and bone-headed that they might be mistaken for an episode of Monty Python or an unusually addled issue of *Mad Magazine*.

To begin with, there was no system of retirement. Not only did senior officers stay in office until senile, blocking any promotion for younger and more vigorous men, but stayed in office even when in a coma. Col. Thomas Lawson had been appointed army surgeon general in 1836. When the Civil War opened he was not only in his eighties but was literally unconscious. But he could not be replaced until he was actually dead. No pulse, no respiration. Stone cold dead. No doubt Lawson, during his twenty-five years in the post as surgeon general, had been familiar with the bizarre notion of the "hospital fund," an army concept so illogical, so penny pinching, so mean and narrow that it vies with the "no retirement" concept for sheer idiocy.

Army policy decreed that each soldier was to receive daily rations worth thirty cents. If he was wounded or sick, and in hospital, he needed only thirteen cents worth of food. The seventeen cents "saved" was to go in the "hospital fund," and was to be used for "delicacies," such as chicken, milk, or vegetables.

The Old Army was scattered across the west in isolated forts, usually just in single companies, with an entire regiment rarely gathered in one spot. A typical fort might have 100 men, a handful of officers and a surgeon. The doctor's duties included more than healing the sick. He was to keep a strict accounting of the hospital funds, with regular reports to Washington, DC. In Godforsaken wastes like the Nevada desert it was not clear how to obtain the "delicacies" noted in many accounting-based courts-martial, but on a small post the actual bookkeeping was not too onerous. However, as the 70,000 men of the Army of the Potomac marched along, scattering wounded and sick in its wake, the concept of the "hospital fund" remained, in all its inane glory, in all its totally unworkable inflexibility.

When Col. Lawson gave up the ghost, the army got a new surgeon general. Would he be a breath of fresh air, a new broom to sweep away the cobwebs of hidebound, Scrooge-like bureaucracy? That new man was Clement A. Finley, a man who had been a toddler when George Washington was still alive. Finley entered military service in 1818. His pre-Civil War history reveals a tendency to hyper-sensitivity and petty jealousies. Army surgeon William Beaumont, the founder of modern gastroenterology, was stationed at Missouri's Jefferson Barracks. Beaumont ordered Finley to report for duty. Finley refused and was court-martialed. In 1847, a Capt. Macrae ordered Finley, now a major, to attend a muster and inspection. Finley refused on grounds that he outranked the captain. Finley was again court-martialed for disobedience. In 1851, another court-martial, Brevet Lt. Col. Braxton Bragg had ordered a sick man to duty. Finley replied that <u>he</u> held a *regular* commission, while Bragg's rank was by brevet only. After a bitter and contentious trial, Finley was booted out of the army but soon reinstated by President Millard Fillmore.

With the Civil War came Finley's chance to be the fabled breath of fresh air, but instead he brought the dead and stifling miasma of the tomb, the nasty and narrow seeking of prerogative. In a series of seven-way administrative battles, Finley took on Dr. Charles S. Tripler, Maj. Gen. George B. McClellan, Secretary of War Simon Cameron, Dr. John Neill (a "prominent member of the medical profession"), Maj. John F. Lee (Judge Advocate of the Army), the Sanitary Commission, and the editors of the powerful *New York Tribune*. Finley lost out and was ordered "retired on disability" in April 1862.

All this discussion of the traditions of the Old Army is a preamble to the subject of the north's equivalent of the south's Brig. Gen. Winder. This man who would be in charge of feeding, clothing, and supplying the Confederate soldiers held in Union POW camps was William Hoffman. His career was very parallel with that of Lawson and Finley, with a long immersion in the customs, regulations, and mind sets of the Old Army.

He graduated from West Point in 1829, and was assigned to duty in Missouri and Kansas. In 1832, he fought in the Black Hawk War and in 1837-1842 in the Second Seminole War. During the Mexican War he fought at Vera Cruz, Cerro Gordo, San Antonio, Contreras, and Churubusco, where he was wounded. He was also involved in action at Chapultepec, Mexico City, and Molino del Rey. For his work at the latter place he was brevetted lieutenant colonel for "gallant and meritorious conduct." Between the Mexican War and the Civil War he served mainly in the west: Missouri, Dakota Territory, California, and Texas. In Texas, he was captured and paroled by the traitorous Brig. Gen. David F. Twiggs, who seized all Federal property in Texas and handed it over to the Confederacy.

In June 1862, he was made Commissary-General of Prisoners, reporting directly to Secretary of War Edwin Stanton. Hoffman then had direct access to the inner halls of power and the blessing of those power holders. He soon began to exercise these new powers. At the Point Lookout prison, Brig. Gen. Gilman Marston was in charge. He asked Hoffman for money to build barracks, since the tents provided little shelter in the bitter winters. Hoffman refused. Marston also requested additional money for food. Hoffman replied that the prisoners were "bountifully supplied with provisions" from food parcels sent by prisoner's families in the south. There is scant evidence for such bounty.

A few vignettes from the Rock Island prison will add to understanding Hoffman. As this prison was being constructed its commandant received a telegram from Hoffman announcing the imminent arrival of 5,000 Confederate prisoners. In spite of the warning that the only water supply on the island was one well and that housing was unfinished, the prisoners arrived. They were already exhausted, having endured a long ride in boxcars provided with no food or water and as crowded and filthy as those carrying victims to Buchenwald and Dachau in a future century. It was winter with snow on the ground and the camp had no clothes or blankets.

On Christmas Eve 1863, Hoffman reduced prisoners' molasses ration from four quarts per 100 men to one quart per 100 men. Things grew worse in March 1864, when a large number of exchanged Union prisoners arrived in the Washington DC area. Both government and civilian officials were horrified at the condition of the men: walking skeletons, blank-eyed, listless, utterly demoralized, shattered husks of men. The cries for retribution were endorsed by Stanton, the blessing that Hoffman needed. On a day that pork was available the new ration was 10 ounces; beef was reduced to 14 ounces per man. Following Hoffman's Old Army fixation on "hospital funds" and "savings," the commandant at Rock Island "saved" $6,500 by selling 24 tons of bread and ten tons of beef back to the commissary. At Rock Island, men who took the Oath of Allegiance (not the galvanized men) were simply put on the Iowa shore in the same ragged clothes in which they had been captured, without food or transportation. The Iowa citizens, who had profited by selling goods and services to the prison, were now horrified to find dozens of Confederates entering the County

Poorhouse, to be fed at Iowa's expense. The prison commandant asked Hoffman's permission to give these indigent and starving men some hardtack. The answer was "no."

One prison commandant requested money to clothe his prisoners. Hoffman replied, "So long as a prisoner has clothing upon him, however much torn, issue nothing to him," cold comfort indeed as the winter winds whistled down out of Canada. Hoffman inspected New York's Fort Lafayette and concluded, "The fort itself furnishes no room for prisoners . . . but some 500 prisoners may be accommodated." Fort Lafayette's new commandant wrote," "The prisoners are entirely destitute of bedding and, in great measure, of the necessary clothing to insure cleanliness and comfort." In brief, men in rags slept on the cold stone floor.

Was there a national food shortage to justify Hoffman's policies? In 1840 the north produced 631 million bushels of grains (wheat, corn, oats, barley, rye, and buckwheat). In 1850, this figure had jumped to 867 million bushels. At the opening of the Civil War the new crop estimates were for 1.4 billion bushels. During the war, with new agricultural machinery coming into use, grain production rose even more, with enough national surplus to create a huge trade to Europe, via New York's harbors.

The Old Army's "hospital fund" lived on in Hoffman's "prison fund." The "savings" from shorting the prisoners on things like hardtack was supposed to be for buying vegetables, but at the end of the war, Hoffman proudly returned $1.8 million to the government. He had not spent the money, roughly $54 million in today's dollars! What would $54 million buy today? The 2015 USDA figures for wholesale carrots suggest that Hoffman could have purchased at least 54 million pounds of carrots, enough to prevent or cure scurvy and night blindness in every soldier in every army, roughly ten pounds of carrots for every soldier between Mexico and Canada, in prison or out. Whether Hoffman did right in starving prisoners in retaliation for conditions in the Confederate prisons is a matter for moralists and ethicists, but it cannot be argued that the north was short of food.

Compared With What?

One of the oldest dialogues in vaudeville involved two comedians. One asked, "How's your wife?" The other replies, "Compared with what?" Here the question is: How was life on active duty, compared with life as a prisoner of war?

Exact figures for the Confederacy are a problem. The pre-eminent student of the armies of the Confederacy and especially the Army of Northern Virginia, Robert K. Krick, makes this analysis. Broadfoot Publishing has computerized all the available compiled military service records of the Confederacy, a total of 1,240,000 records. Because many men served in several units, thus generating several set of records, the number of actual men must be adjusted. Based on a literal life-time of studying these records, Krick estimates that 25 percent of the 1,240,000 records represent the same man, concluding that roughly 90,000 individual served in the southern armies. An educated guess as to total casualties from disease and wounds is 275,000, yielding a mortality rate of 30.6 percent.

How does this compare with the mortality as a prisoner of war? Exact numbers from the Union POW camps are hard to find, but using the highest figures from a variety of sources, the largest camps had these mortality rates: Elmira (25%); Camp Douglas (23%); Rock Island (17%); Point Lookout (8%). The combined experience of these four large camps suggests an overall mortality rate of 18.3%. On a statistical basis, it was safer to be in a Union POW camp than to serve on active duty in Confederate forces..

True, life in the prison camps was miserable and the survivors were often in shattered physical and mental condition, but years on active service with long marches, bad food, poor clothing, often shoeless, with at least one episode of severe dysentery each year would also yield a much depleted man.

The Union figures are derived from Frederick M. Dyer's *Compendium of the War of the Rebellion*. All Federal military men, including white troops, colored troops, Indian troops, and Navy personnel, totaled 2,778,304. Union dead, from all causes, totaled 359,528, a mortality of 12.9 percent. How did Union men fare in Confederate captivity? This question is made difficult by gaps in the Confederate records. Best estimates of mortality rates for three major Confederate facilities are: Andersonville (30%); Camp Lawton (22%); and the Florence Stockade (17%), with an overall rate of 23%.

Granted the great difficulties in drawing meaningful conclusions from these figures, three findings seem likely. (1) By a small margin, a prisoner was more likely to die in a Confederate camp than in a Union camp; (2) A Union prisoner was twice as likely to die as a prisoner than serving on active duty; and (3) a Confederate soldier was more likely to die on active service than in a Union prison camp.

A general conclusion is easy to make: neither north nor south was prepared to house, feed, and clothe large numbers of prisoners, nor was either side willing to make much effort to alleviate the well-documented and often-fatal deprivations.

With this background discussion on prison mortality, we pass on to other factors that shaped the lives of Virginia men who galvanized into Union service, with a brief digression upon the diseases of malnutrition.

CHAPTER 4
THE PRISONS

Most of the Confederate soldiers who galvanized into the United States Volunteers had been held in one of five Union prison camps: Point Lookout; Rock Island; Camp Douglas; Morton; or Alton.

Point Lookout

Maryland is an oddly-shaped state: wide in its western mountains and eastern shore, but narrow in its middle. Part of eastern Maryland is a long peninsula, terminating in a narrow point, bounded on the west by the mouth of the Potomac River and on the east by the Chesapeake Bay. The terrain on the point is flat, fertile, and sandy, with foul and brackish ground water. The point got its name in the War of

1812, when American spies noted the movement of British vessels and sent the intelligence to Washington, DC, by relays of horses.

The coming of the Civil War changed the point into a busy port and added the Hammond Hospital, a large facility with fifteen long buildings radiating out from a central point, like the spokes of a wheel. An influx of Confederate prisoners after the Battle of Gettysburg added another activity: a prison camp. During its 1863-1865 existence, more than 50,000 men passed through its gates. The prisoners were housed in tents, which gave little protection from the winter winds. Many men wore only the thin and threadbare clothes in which they had marched barefoot through Pennsylvania's July heat. The winter of 1863-1864 was unusually severe, there was no firewood, and many men froze to death. The legions of lice, the scanty rations, and the endless boredom took their toll. Especially grievous to the Southerners were the guards from the US Colored Troops; many had been slaves and relished their new power. Prisoners wrote in their diaries of men cramping with diarrhea, staggering toward the sinks (latrine trenches), who were shot for being out of their tents at night. Although the death toll was less than many Civil War prison camps, it was still a miserable existence.

Rock Island

The Mississippi River forms the border between Iowa and Illinois. Leave Chicago on Interstate 80, drive 170 miles straight west, and you'll be on the banks of the Mississippi. In the middle of the river is an island two miles long and a half mile wide. This is Rock Island.

The Quartermaster-General, Montgomery Meigs, set the tone for Rock Island's prison facility: "The barracks for prisoners at Rock Island should be put up in the roughest and cheapest manner. Mere shanties, with no fine work about them." (Of course, when the green lumber dried and contracted, the wind whistled through.) Altogether, 84 prison barracks were built, each 100 by 22 feet. Though "rough" and "cheap," they were certainly superior to Point Lookout's tents. Unlike most other prisons, there was a surplus of food: beef, fresh-baked bread, and other nutritious items. This was near Paradise—good food and new barracks. The bubble burst soon enough.

In December 1863, 5,000 Confederate soldiers captured at Chattanooga were put in over-crowded cars, with no food or water, and started for Rock Island. When Commissary-General of Prisoners William Hoffman telegraphed the camp commander, he replied that the barracks and, even more important the water supply, were not yet ready. The men arrived anyway, starving, sick, thirsty, and shivering in the cold. The remaining years of the war saw a succession of camp commanders, political and monetary intrigue on the part of the surrounding town's businessmen, and an extra array of dreadful camp guards. First rate soldiers were sent to fight; the leftovers guarded prison camps.

First, there was Invalid Corps, later termed the Veteran Reserve Corps. At Rock Island prison, these men spent more time drinking and whoring than guarding. They were frequently court-martialed for offenses such as seizing a saloon in a nearby town and telling the sheriff, "You'll never take us alive." In time came replacements: the Graybeard Regiment, formally the 37th Iowa Infantry, Col. George W. Kincaid, commanding. These were elderly men, whose age and wisdom would be a stabilizing force, ideal for guard duty. The reality was somewhat different. One soldier wrote home that the entire camp was "covered in the greatest effusions of snot that human eyes have ever beheld." (Not exactly sharp soldiers.) While kinder than some of the previous guards, the elders, who preferred to raise their own bacon rather than eat the second-rate pork from crooked Federal contractors, bedeviled the camp commander with their personal herd of swine. Their main contention was with their martinet colonel, whom they openly despised.

The next attempt to recruit camp guards were the Hundred Day regiments, attempts to lure men into brief service. The 133rd Illinois Infantry, on its way to Rock Island by train, desecrated so many villages during brief stops that the colonel was soon busy writing letters of apology. Once on duty, the "Hundred Dazers" took to shooting prisoners, nearby civilians, and each other. When the laundresses were removed from the barracks of the 133rd Illinois, the soldiers turned to self-help, and two men were court-martialed for masturbation. (In the 1860s, both medical and lay opinion held that what Mark Twain called a "majestic diversion" was non-military, potentially fatal, and certainly contrary to Holy Writ.) This unruly bunch of hundred-day men was then replaced by the 108th US Colored Troops, who were just as happy to shoot prisoners as had been their predecessors. Added to the deliberately reduced rations in the last year of the war, Rock Island was a dreadful place.

The recruitment of men who might wish to galvanize introduced yet another tension to the island. Those swearing allegiance to the United States had to be segregated, as the loyal Confederates cursed and threatened them. Rock Island was yet one more variant in the spectrum of Civil War prison camps and their miseries.

Camp Douglas

South of Chicago was another large prison camp. The area was first used as a training camp for new Illinois troops, who left it in such damaged shape that it needed repairs to hold Confederate prisoners for a few months, before returning to its original use for trainees. From January 1863 to May 1865, the area was devoted solely to housing prisoners of war. During this period the camp had at least seven different commanders, each with his own style of management.

From the beginning, in spite of numerous recommendations by visiting inspectors, the camp's housing and water systems were inadequate and tended to stay that way. A sewer system was not even authorized, much less constructed, until June 1863. As early as July 1862, the US

Sanitary Commission had strongly suggested abandoning the site, as it was hopelessly inundated with feces, ground water, and rotting garbage. Federal officials, including Quartermaster General Meigs, objected to most improvements as "extravagant," and moved only under political pressure.

The real story of the prison began January 26, 1863, with arrival of 1,500 poorly clothed, starving, and sick Confederates. In the following week, another 2,800 men arrived. The facilities were immediately overwhelmed. The weather was bitter cold. The camp commander telegraphed Washington, informing his superiors that many of these men were too weak to stand the harsh conditions, but his plea was largely ignored. In February 1863, 387 prisoners died.

The next two years saw more camp commanders, many escapes, endless tunneling, removal of the barracks floors to reveal possible tunnels, contractor scandals, corrupt guards, and shooting of prisoners. In January 1864's blizzard, temperatures dropped to minus 18 degrees F. The camp commander obtained some surplus overcoats for his prisoners, but was reprimanded by Col. Hoffman for proceeding outside the required bureaucratic channels.

By 1864 the prison hospital overflowed. Many were weakened by scurvy, a result of Col. Hoffman's refusal to send vegetables to the prison. In addition to those in the hospital, over 800 were sick in the barracks. An unscrupulous undertaker made a profit by dumping bodies instead of shipping them to their homes.

An exact toll will never be known, but the best estimates are as follows. Roughly 4,454 Confederate prisoners died at Camp Douglas, with a mortality rate of 17 percent.

Camp Morton

Oliver Morton was governor of Indiana during the Civil War. The prison camp, built on the state fairgrounds near Indianapolis, bore his name. In late February 1862, it received its first inmates; when the camp closed in June 1865, approximately 1,700 prisoners had died there, a mortality rate reported as 12.5 percent. As the war went on the usual problems of overcrowding and poor maintenance overwhelmed attempts at decent care. A medical inspector in October 1863 noted sufficient food, clothing, and water, but criticized the dilapidated and poorly maintained buildings, lax discipline, and bad drainage. By the summer of 1864, the prison held almost 5,000 men. Some drama was injected in July 1863, with Gen. John Hunt Morgan's cavalry sweep across the Midwest. Whether this bold expedition helped the Confederacy is open to debate, but it did add 1,100 prisoners to the Camp Morton roster.

The Confederate dead were buried in several locations. After the war, families retrieved nearly 100 bodies for re-burial at home, leaving roughly 1,600 men still in Greenlawn Cemetery. The following year a fire in the cemetery office destroyed the records of burial locations. After several intervening moves, the remains were finally gathered in a mass grave in Section 32 of Crown Hill Cemetery, where they remain today.

The overall history of Camp Morton suggests that it was a safer and more humane facility than most Civil War prison camps. The first commandant of the camp, Col. Richard Owen, was noted for his kindness and concern, so much so that after the war a group of former Confederate prisoners erected a monument to him. There is no record of such an effort by former prisoners of Andersonville.

Alton Prison

In movies about Chicago gangsters, the criminals often speak of "doing hard time at Joliet." Yet Joliet was the replacement for Illinois' first (and far worse) prison, built at Alton. Completed in 1831 and later condemned as "unsanitary" and "undrained," its last convicts were shipped to Joliet in 1860. Just in time for the Civil War.

This condemned and abandoned facility, built of heavy limestone blocks and resembling a medieval castle, was now deemed perfectly suitable for prisoners of war. Lieut. Col. James B. McPherson reported that it could be made appropriate for 1,750 prisoners for a mere $2,415. Starting in February 1862, a total of 11,764 Confederate prisoners would pass through its portals. A smallpox epidemic in the winter of 1862-1863 caused the creation of a Pest House on a nearby island, where nearly 300 died. (The island was washed away by floods years ago.) Pneumonia, measles, and dysentery took their usual toll, abetted by chronic malnutrition. The best available death records list 1,534 Confederate soldiers, suggesting a death rate of 13 percent.

This brief overview of Union prisons suggests why a Confederate soldier might consider galvanizing and wearing Union blue. Was it the thought of fighting small bands of Indians, rather than charging into cannons belching canister? Was it the hopes of improved diet? Was it the possibility of clothing superior to the tattered rags worn by most of the prisoners? Was it some hope of the sanitation of a small western fort, a post not running with raw sewage like so many of the POW camps? Or perhaps a fading hope of a successful Confederacy? It may be impossible to discover these men's thoughts today, but all of the above may have played a part.

Nota bene. Several excellent sources more deeply document the stories of these prisons.

Lonnie R. Speer: *Portals to Hell.* Bison Books, University of Nebraska Press, 2005.

George Levy: *To Die in Chicago.* Pelican Publishing, 1999.

Richard H. Triebe: *Point Lookout.* Coastal Books, 2014.

Benton McAdams: *Rebels at Rock Island.* Northern Illinois University Press, 2000.

Robert C. Jones: *Civil War Prison Camps.* Jone442@bellsouth.net, 2011.

CHAPTER 5
SCURVY AND NIGHT BLINDNESS

Scurvy

  Most readers today associate the word "scurvy" with old pirate movies, where the captain, with wooden leg and eye patch, shouts, "Avast, ye scurvy dogs!" Yet this disease, once the killer of tens of thousands, is never very far from us. The author was an intern at the county hospital in Minneapolis in 1957. A man in late middle age came in to be treated for "varicose veins." My fellow intern, Ernie Thorsgaard, a laconic and intuitive former dairy farmer, thought the purple lesions didn't look right and ordered a blood ascorbic acid level. It was very low. A hundred milligrams of Vitamin C daily cured all the man's symptoms. He had scurvy, the result of living in a transient hotel, subsisting on a nearly vitamin-free diet.

It was only until the past generation that all the chemistry and physiology of scurvy has been clarified, but its recognition as a cluster of symptoms goes back at least three thousand years. The Ebers Papyrus, 1500 BCE, described the symptoms well and recommended onions as a cure. Hippocrates described the symptoms as fetid breath, lax gums, and violent nose bleeds. The Age of Exploration, with long voyages and non-availability of fresh food, produced medical disasters. On Vasco de Gama's first trip, 100 of his 160 men died of scurvy. Magellan lost 125 of his 250 men to scurvy. In the Seven Years War, the British Navy lost 120,000 men to scurvy. Jacques Cartier, when his ships were icebound in Canada, had only three men well out of his entire crew, and many dead. Cartier, unlike some explorers, had the good sense to consult the native people. They advised a tea made of the needles of the Eastern White Cedar. Within days, Cartier's remaining men were cured. In 1614, the surgeon-general of the East India Company recommended oranges and lemons as treatment for scurvy. Certainly, the prevalence and cures of this disease were no secret, yet the mechanisms of illness and cure remained obscure until within living memory, for reasons to be discussed shortly.

Today, the word "scurvy" elicits little fear in the minds of readers, but a look at the symptoms and prognosis of the condition should induce more respect for scurvy and, if properly understood, a sense of horror. First, if untreated, the outcome is, invariably, death. And a horrible death it is. The early symptoms include weakness, lack of energy, bone pain, and extreme fatigue. These symptoms first appear after roughly two months without a source of Vitamin C. Then come the truly destructive changes, and they mostly have to do with collagen.

Collagen is the tough, fibrous tissue which makes up tendons, ligaments, the periosteum (fibrous wrapping of the bones), and the bands of tissue which anchor the teeth into the jawbones. Things start to fall apart. Teeth become loose in their sockets. The gums enlarge and bleed. The breath becomes increasingly foul. Defective connective tissue weakens blood vessels, even the tiny capillaries. Mucous membranes in the nose and throat begin to bleed. The legs become blotched with blood leaking from disintegrating veins. As the condition progresses, the stricken man lies immobile, in ever-increasing pain, deeply depressed, teeth gone, open draining wounds leaking foul liquid, the skin yellow from a dying liver, and finally he dies.

Why was it not until the 1930s that the underlying chemistry, and consequent effective treatment was clarified? It looked as though James Lind, a surgeon with the Royal Navy, had settled the matter in his book *A Treatise of the Scurvy*, published in 1753. He described his experiments of treating scurvy with fresh citrus fruits. While the Navy ignored his findings for decades, they began to issue lime or lemon juice on a daily basis, along with the traditional tot of rum. However, the process of boiling the juice in order to preserve it actually destroyed the Vitamin C. What wasn't killed by boiling was further degraded by being kept in copper pots. Physicians at the time did not understand that boiled lime juice was not equivalent to fresh lime juice. Some researchers believed that ascorbic acid was effective because it was acidic, and concluded that any acid would do. Many wrong assumptions confused the issue of scurvy for over a century.

The French encountered scurvy during the 1801 Siege of Alexandria, Egypt, and found that fresh horse meat would cure scurvy. (Most animals can synthesize their own ascorbic acid; humans cannot.) During the Napoleonic Wars, the British Navy turned to issuing fresh lemons. Scurvy dropped to near zero.

Fresh meat will treat scurvy; canned ("tinned") meat will not, due to the heat used in the canning process. British expeditions using canned meat developed scurvy. This led to a dead end in thinking, i.e., scurvy was caused by a "ptomaine" in canned meat. In 1907, two Norwegian physicians, Axel Holst and Theodor Frølich, clearly showed that scurvy was caused by a diet deficient in fresh vegetables. In 1927, Hungarian biochemist Albert Szent-Györgyi isolated hexuronic acid, later termed ascorbic acid.

How does all this relate to the Civil War? First, a look at what foods, in normal portions, provide Vitamin C. (The recommended daily dose is 60 mg. per day.) Fresh lemon: 240 mg. Raw potato: 30 mg. Cooked potato: 10 mg. Raw onion: 20 mg. Cooked onion: 3 mg. Rice: zero. Wheat bread: zero. Most

Civil War soldiers never saw a fresh lemon. Johnny Rebs and Billy Yanks were more likely to get hard tack and salt pork. The result was scurvy. They knew intuitively that they needed vegetables, and they would strip an orchard of fruit or a field of green corn or a cellar of potatoes, not just for vandalism and theft, but to keep alive. On Sherman's March through Georgia the troops would strip every berry from a huge patch of blackberries. What the soldiers knew intuitively seemed to escape the administrators in Washington.

It was not merely pig-headedness that kept the troops on the verge of scurvy. Providing fresh vegetables to 70,000 men on the march is not easy. The roads were narrow and unpaved. They were seas of mud in the winter and dust storms in the summer. Railroads were not always nearby. A commander, forced to choose between a wagonload of ammunition and a wagonload of vegetables, will choose the ammunition. The answer was "dessicated, compressed mixed vegetables," mandated by Congress. The regulations specified string beans, turnips, carrots, beets, and onions. The soldiers hated them, dubbed them "desecrated vegetables," and claimed that the contents were actually roots, leaves, and stalks. Considering the carnival of fraud perpetrated by crooked contractors, the soldiers may have been correct. The dessicated vegetables were dried and compressed into cakes ten inches square and an inch thick. They needed to be boiled to separate the contents. With boiling, volume increased to a startling degree. The final criterion, taste, was not a success.

The soldiers hated them. And the boiling destroyed most of the Vitamin C.

The exact number of Union troops suffering from scurvy is unknown, because only cases requiring hospitalization were reported. In 1865, the rate of scurvy among Union white troops was 4.2 cases per thousand men. The true incidence was probably far higher.

The galvanized Yankees served mainly in isolated forts along the frontier, with nary a lemon tree or the fields full of the vegetables we now take for granted. Did the steamboats coming up the Missouri River carry anti-scorbutics of any sort? That crucial question will be answered in subsequent chapters.

Night Blindness

Thou hast eyes, but seeth not, paraphrased from Job 10:4. At night, the native people could see; the soldiers could not. The Plains Indians fell into two general groupings. The more eastern tribes grew crops: maize, squash, beans, and sunflowers, supplemented with venison. The more westerly tribes lived on buffalo meat, fresh after a hunt, or dried into jerky for later use. The sedentary tribes traded vegetables for jerky. Both groups achieved a balanced diet. The soldiers, as we have seen, lived on hardtack, which not only lacked Vitamin C but also a nutrient vital for vision, especially night vision.

Today, there are nearly a dozen known causes of night blindness, including retinitis pigmentosa, cataracts, and surgical injuries, but none of these applied to the young soldiers manning the forts. They lacked Vitamin A, which is found in abundance in sweet potatoes, squash, and carrots. (It is also found in kale, Romaine lettuce, dried apricots, cantaloupe, sweet red peppers, and tuna, none of which were in evidence at the army's western forts.)

The human retina contains ten layers, all in a space less than a millimeter thick. There are two types of light receptive cells: the rods, active in the dark, and the cones, which serve daytime vision. One of the essential factors in retinal function is retinol, which is produced in the retina from Vitamin A, which in turn is derived from dietary beta-carotene. The complexity of sight is illustrated in the following quotation from the Wikipedia article on rhodopsin, and suggests that retinal function was not only a mystery to frontier surgeons but is certainly a challenge to most non-specialists today.

"Rhodopsin consists of the protein moiety opsin and a reversibly covalently bound co-factor, retinal. Opsin, a bundle of seven transmembrane helices connected to each other by polypeptide loops, binds retinal (a photoreactive chromophore), which is located in a central pocket on the seventh helix at a lysine residue."

The shortages of both Vitamin C and Vitamin A can explain the success of night-time Indian raids, which made off with the post's livestock. Many of the soldiers were deathly ill with scurvy, unable to eat their only food –

hardtack – because of rotting gums and failing teeth and if they ventured out at night to fend off attack, unable to see.

The tribulations of George C. Potts, surgeon with the 23rd US Colored Troops, may suggest the army's willingness to provide proper nutrition. As soon as Lee had surrendered, this regiment was shipped to Brazos de Santiago, a dreadful spot on the southern border of Texas. There they quickly developed scurvy and within weeks half the regiment was too sick for duty. Potts' correspondence with his medical and administrative superiors, detailing the sufferings of his men and the need for better food, was greeted with derision. His own regimental commander considered him a madman and a troublemaker. Help finally came from an unlikely source: Maj. Gen. Philip Sheridan interceded and ordered that Potts' post be provided with vegetables.

Will the same help come for the galvanized Yankees in their frontier posts?

CHAPTER 6
THE GEOGRAPHY

———————————————

Most students of the Civil War, both amateur and professional, are familiar with the war sites of Pennsylvania, Virginia, and the Carolinas. Moving west past the Blue Ridge Mountains, the geography is quickly less familiar, and further west, beyond the Mississippi and Missouri, America's truly great rivers, most Civil War buffs must resort to maps, websites, and reference works. Even the familiar maps posted on the walls of most grammar school rooms are no help, because the dotted lines imposed upon the landscapes have changed many times.

To the galvanized Virginia soldiers, both the topography and the political boundaries were great unknowns. This effort to bring clarity out of the mists of time begins with the states in which they would serve. Kansas, the site of bloody warfare between abolitionists and slavery advocates, and their proxy armies of jayhawkers and bushwhackers, was admitted as a state in January 1861. Oklahoma, which existed for years as Indian Territory, has an extraordinarily complex history. By the time of the Civil War it contained not only the Choctaw and Cherokee people, expelled from their native lands by Andrew Jackson, but nearly twenty other Native American tribes and nations. The great north-bound cattle drives passed through Indian Territory, creating new sources of friction. Reflecting its internal conflicts, Oklahoma was not admitted as a state until 1907.

Nebraska, created as a territory in 1854, was part of the pre-war conflict involving the Kansas-Nebraska Act, the changes in the Missouri Compromise, and the other maneuverings of the ongoing struggle between the free states and the slave states. Nebraska was admitted to the Union as a state in 1867.

Dakota Territory (1861-1889) included parts of today's North Dakota, South Dakota, Wyoming, and Montana. A battalion of Dakota Territory Cavalry served in the Union army. Today's states of North and South Dakota were admitted to the Union in 1889. Colorado Territory was assembled from parts of the territories of Utah, Kansas, New Mexico, and Nebraska, and was admitted to the Union as a state in its current configuration in 1876. The Colorado Volunteers were vital in turning back Sibley's Confederate invasion of the southwest.

Montana was another state created by conjoining parts of other territories: Oregon; Washington; Idaho; and Dakota. It achieved statehood in 1889.

The Rivers

To the Indians, settlers, and soldiers who traversed these vast domains, the state and territory boundary lines were fictions. The lines cut across mountain ranges; they ignored river drainage basins; they bore no connection to climatic zones. The features of the land had existed for millennia, long before today's network of freeways and railroads. In the mid-1800s the clearest features of the landscape were the rivers. Once again, to Civil War buffs, the well-known rivers were the Anna, Potomac, and James Rivers, but from Ohio to California the other rivers, America's great rivers, are more of a mystery. Here they are, described as related to today's political boundaries, beginning of course, at New Orleans. Put a paddle in the waters of Ole Miss and start north.

The first great confluence is roughly 120 miles north where the Red River debouches into the Mississippi. The Red arises in eastern New Mexico, flows across the northern portion of Texas, and then forms the border between Texas and Oklahoma. After a brief turn through southwest Arkansas, it ends near Simmesport, Louisiana, in a complex intermingling of the Red, Mississippi and Atchafalaya Rivers.

The next great river to enter the Mississippi is the Arkansas, whose total length is 700 miles. It arises in the mountains of Colorado, and flows southeast across Kansas, where its most northerly point is Great Bend. It then turns southeast across Oklahoma and into Arkansas where it joins the Mississippi near Little Rock. The Arkansas River has two major tributaries, the Cimarron and the Canadian Rivers, which run roughly parallel to it. Each tributary is about fifty miles south of the course of the Arkansas itself. The Cimarron arises in northeast New Mexico, flows through Oklahoma and enters the Arkansas near Tulsa. The Canadian also begins in northeast New Mexico, runs parallel to the Cimarron, and enters the Arkansas between Muscogee and Fort Smith. There is a Little Arkansas River. It rises in Rice County, Kansas, and flows 123 miles southeast to join the Arkansas at Wichita.

Next riverine event of note is the junction of the Mississippi and Ohio Rivers, at Cairo, Illinois. Cairo today is an impoverished backwater, but during the Civil War it was a very busy military port. The Ohio begins its 981-mile course in eastern Pennsylvania, forms the northern borders of Kentucky and West Virginia, and is today jammed with barge traffic.

Three hundred miles upstream from Cairo is the great junction, where at St. Louis, Missouri, the Mississippi (bound north to Minnesota) is joined by the Mighty Missouri. In the era of steamboats, even with all its snags and shifting sand bars, the Missouri, angling its way ever to the northwest, was the gateway to the frontier. The first major inflowing stream is the Platte, entering the Missouri from the west about 400 miles upstream from St. Louis.

The Platte, little known to Americans on either coast, was very important in opening the west. It was too shallow for navigation but its banks during its long meandering toward the setting sun were ideal for wagon trains and, later, railroads. Along its gentle slopes trod the emigrants using the Oregon, California, Mormon, and Bozeman Trails. (Its shallow waters are host each Spring to an enormous migration of sand hill cranes. In March the motels are full of birdwatchers and the river is full of birds.) The river has two major branches. The North Platte has its origin in Wyoming, while the South Platte begins near Denver. The two converge shortly after entering Nebraska; the full stream of the Platte enters the Missouri at Omaha. A few hundred miles further north, the Niobrara River enters from the west, near the border of Nebraska and South Dakota. Another powerful subsidiary, the Cheyenne River, enters from the west in the middle of South Dakota. At Williston, North Dakota, now a wild oil town, the Missouri turns straight west. A few miles on, the powerful Yellowstone River adds its flow, and in Montana the Milk River and the Marias River, so prominent in the diaries of Lewis and Clark, make their contributions.

The galvanized Virginians are about to see a land so vast, with rivers so powerful, that the gentle Shenandoah, despite its grasp upon their hearts, even with its legends, even with the talons of nostalgia and homesickness hard upon them, will feel both the terror and exhilaration of agoraphobia.

The Trails

While the extensive trail system that traversed the West was manmade, it was in some ways natural. Many of the trails originated as buffalo migration trails. The Indians followed the same trails and the first white men to arrive saw no reason to do differently. Modern highways and powerful engines enable travelers today to fly over canyons and cut through mountains, but to men and beasts on foot, the natural contours of the land dictate the route. At least five major trails live on in history.

The Oregon Trail

The Oregon Trail jumping-off spots were Council Bluffs, Iowa and Independence, Missouri. These two branches united at Grand Island, Nebraska, and continued west along the Platte. At today's town of North Platte the river forked and the trail followed the North Platte, passing Courthouse Rock, Chimney Rock, Scott's Bluff and on to where the Sweetwater River joins the North Platte. The trail then followed the Sweetwater to its headwaters at South Pass, the lowest spot in the Rockies. From here, the usual route proceeded to Fort Bridger in Wyoming, then northward to Fort Hall, Idaho, then onwards west via Fort Boise, passing beyond the purview of our galvanized Yankees.

The California Trail

The California Trail followed the same route as the Oregon Trail until branching off near Fort Hall. Crossing the northeast tip of Nevada, the California followed the Humboldt River until the water sank into the desert. After a forty-mile waterless stretch the travelers reached Carson City. From there, four different trails led over the Sierras into California's Central Valley.

The Mormon Trail

Once again, these travelers moved along the North Platte and Sweetwater rivers, over South Pass and on to Fort Bridger. There, they turned southwest until they reached Salt Lake City.

The Bozeman Trail

This route followed the Oregon Trail until just west of Fort Laramie, when it headed northwest to Fort Reno, Wyoming. From there it passed the site of the Fetterman Massacre, thence to Forts C. F. Smith and Ellis in Montana, then on to the gold fields.

The Santa Fé Trail

The northern portions of this trail formed part of the galvanized Virginian's experience. The Santa Fé also began at Independence, Missouri, and angled west-southwest across Kansas, with major stations at Council Grove and Diamond Spring. Next came Fort Zarah, situated on the Great Bend of the Arkansas River, then on to Fort Dodge, where the trail split into two routes. The Mountain Route continued west, along the Arkansas River to Fort Lyon and Bent's Fort in Colorado, then turned south, crossing the New Mexico border at Raton, turning straight south to Wagon Mound, Las Vegas (the New Mexico Las Vegas), and Santa Fé.

The Cimarron Route departed from the Arkansas River, heading southwest. The first barrier was the Cimarron River itself. At least two fords were used to cross the river, both recorded as the Cimarron Crossing. In southwest Kansas the trail passed Lower Spring and the wagons often paused at Willow Bar in southeast Colorado. From there the trail crossed the far west end of the Oklahoma panhandle, joining the Mountain Route at Fort Union and Las Vegas, both in New Mexico.

In the long stretches between forts, the travelers were subjected to heat, cold, dust, cholera, dysentery, and Indians. While the US Volunteers could do nothing about the far more dangerous weather and disease, they were expected to do something about the Indians, who, of course, saw their lands as being invaded and stolen.

CHAPTER 7

THE FORTS

The US Volunteers served at a dozen or more locations, in addition to their times of travel and expeditions away from military posts. They rarely served as complete regiments, but were often scattered in separate companies. Here are those known locations, presented in alphabetical order. Locations are described using modern boundaries as reference points.

Fort Abercrombie was built in 1858 on the Red River of the North, in North Dakota. In 1862 it survived a six-week siege by Sioux.

Fort Berthold was on the left bank of the Missouri River, in upper North Dakota, just below the mouth of the Little Missouri River. It was built in 1858 by a fur trading company and first named Fort Atkinson. (The location was near the Mandan and Hidatsa villages, where Lewis and Clark spent one winter.) In 1864 the 6th Iowa Cavalry was sent to Fort Berthold after Indian attacks. Following a quarrel with the fur traders, the Army built its own post just outside the original stockade. It reverted to being a trading post and Indian agency headquarters in 1867 when the soldiers moved to Fort Stevenson twelve miles downstream. The location is now under the waters of the Garrison Reservoir.

Fort Cottonwood (see Fort McPherson).

Dodge City is a place known to any fan of Western movies and books. This once-wild cow town is located in the southwest corner of Kansas. It takes its name from Fort Dodge which was a few miles west of the city. The fort was established in September 1865 to protect the Santa Fé Trail, and was situated on the left bank of the Arkansas River between the Mulberry Creek Crossing and the Cimarron Crossing. It was probably named after Col. Henry Dodge of the 1st Dragoons. It was abandoned in 1882, but until recently two of the old adobe buildings housed the Fort Dodge Soldier's Home.

Elm Creek is mentioned frequently in the records of the US Volunteers. It is located in today's Buffalo County, in south central Nebraska. In 2010 its population was 901.

Fort Ellsworth was established in 1864. Today, the word "fort" conjures up visions of turrets, towers, cannon embrasures, and moats. The Old West was a low-budget operation. Ellsworth was built on the banks of the Smokey

Hill River in today's Ellsworth County, Kansas. The location was at a ford on the road from Fort Riley to Fort Larned. A few buildings were put up during the Civil War, but in January 1865 troops were still living in dugouts with mud chimneys. As to security, in August 1864, Indians captured most of the post and stage companies' horses and mules, leaving behind only two horses. Five months later only seven of the horses had been replaced. In 1866, the post was renamed Fort Harker, and in 1867 the entire facility was moved to a new site a mile away.

Fort Halleck was located near today's Elk Mountain, Wyoming. It was established in 1862 to guard the Overland Trail. When most active, it had stable space for 200 horses.

Fort Harker, which had actual fortifications, was one of the most important military posts west of the Missouri River. Its site near Kanopolis, in central Kansas, still has many of the original buildings, carefully preserved by the Ellsworth County Historical Society. Until the Indian Wars moved farther west, it was a major supply post. The railroad arrived in 1867, carrying with it cholera, which filled the post's cemetery. The fort was abandoned in 1872.

Fort Larned. The Pawnee River, often referred to as Pawnee Fork, is a branch of the Arkansas River running through central Kansas. As the tribes, including the Kiowa, Apache, Comanche, Arapaho, and Cheyenne, saw their lands being invaded by the whites, they became increasingly active in attacking the numerous commercial wagons on the Santa

Fé Trail. In 1859, 2,300 men, 190 wagons, 840 horses, 4,000 mules, 15,000 oxen, 73 carriages, and 1,900 tons of freight departed from Missouri, bound for New Mexico. What became Fort Larned was established in 1859 to protect this trade. It was situated near both the "dry route," of the trail, along the Pawnee Fork, and the "wet route," which more closely followed the Arkansas River. Not all the Indians were intimidated by the presence of the army. In July 1864, Kiowas raided Fort Larned and made off with 172 horses and mules. The raiders were never caught. Over its 19 years of operation, 24 different units were stationed there including, in 1865, the 2nd US Volunteer Infantry, galvanized men. In 1868, the adobe buildings were replaced by more elegant sandstone structures. The facility was taken over by the National Park Service in 1964.

Fort Leavenworth. In March 1828, Col. Henry Leavenworth was ordered to select a site for a fort on the left bank of the Missouri River, within twenty miles of the Little Platte River, which flows across the northwest corner of Missouri and is not to be confused with the much larger Platte River of Nebraska. The site first gained prominence as a rendezvous spot for troops heading to the Mexican War. From then to the Civil War, it was the main depot for US military operations in the west. During the war it was a training station for new Union recruits. For the following thirty years it was the army's central base in the Indian War. The coming of the railroads signaled its change from a combat footing to a training and administrative post.

Fort McPherson, known in most records as Fort Cottonwood, was on the North Platte River in Nebraska. Cottonwood Canyon was a twenty-mile-long fertile area through the hills south of the river. It was a favorite crossing location for Indians traveling north and south. There was also a year-round spring where the canyon met the river. The fort was built in the winter of 1862-1863, following the Dakota War, and was abandoned in 1880. It is still the site of Fort McPherson National Cemetery.

Fort Rice, North Dakota, was built about ten miles north of where the Cannonball River enters the Missouri River, thirty miles south of today's city of Mandan. (Other sources describe the location as "near the mouth of Long Lake Creek.") It was established in July 1864 during the campaign against the Sioux. The original facility was log buildings with earth roofs, but was rebuilt in 1868 with better materials. Its stockade was roughly 500 feet square. The site was abandoned in 1878 and its functions moved to Fort Yates. Over the years, the Missouri River has moved, leaving the site several hundred yards from the water. In the autumn of 1864, six companies of the 1st US Volunteers (Galvanized Yankees) arrived to replace the Wisconsin soldiers, and in 1865 two companies of the 4th US Volunteers arrived as reinforcements. During the fort's first year, seven men were killed in combat, but seventy-four died of disease: thirty-seven from scurvy, twenty-four from diarrhea, three of typhoid fever, and the rest of assorted other illnesses.

Fort Ridgely, founded in 1853 in south-central Minnesota, was vital in the Dakota wars of 1862.

Fort Ripley, built in 1849, was located on the banks of the Mississippi River in what is now Minnesota's Crow Wing County.

Fort Riley, Kansas, is the home of the First Infantry Division today. The fort was established in May 1853, on the north bank of the Kansas River, close to the junction of the Smoky Hill and Republican Rivers. The permanent facilities were under construction in August 1855 when cholera killed the post commander and about a hundred other men. Custer's famous 7th US Cavalry was formed at Fort Riley in 1866. In 1867, cholera returned and made further contributions to the post cemetery.

Fort Scott was first established on its site on the eastern border of Kansas, on the Marmaton River, in 1842. Its purpose was to protect the Indians and the settlers from each other. Construction was slow due to shortages of both materials and skilled labor. By the time the buildings were up, the army's priorities had changed and the post was abandoned, only to be reactivated in 1861 with the coming of the war. Troops from Indiana, Iowa, Colorado, Ohio, and Wisconsin passed through the fort, on their way to fight Indians or Confederates. Most of the civilians at Fort Scott were pro-slavery and local conflicts produced murder and arson. Confederate Gen. Sterling Price's invasion came within ten miles of the fort's huge supply of military stores, but was turned back at the Battle of Dry Wood Creek. In 1865, the army abandoned the post; in 1978 the restored buildings came under the stewardship of the National Park Service.

Fort Sedgwick, also known as Julesburg Station and Camp Rankin, was established in May 1864 on the right bank of the South Platte River, near the present-day town of Julesburg, Colorado. It was unusual in having been established by galvanized troops, the 3rd US Volunteers, under Col. Christopher H. McNally. Its purpose was to protect emigrants using nearby river crossings of the Overland Trail. The post was abandoned in 1871. The land is now privately owned. Only a small historic marker remains; there is nothing to be seen of the adobe barracks and hospital.

Fort Union Trading Post, in North Dakota, (not to be confused with Fort Union, New Mexico) is unique in having been established at the request of Indians, in this case, the Assiniboine. It was built near the confluence of the Yellowstone and Missouri Rivers, in 1829. It was never an army post, but was a commercial enterprise and the most active fur trading post on the upper Missouri. The 30th Wisconsin Infantry was stationed there 1864-1865 to protect military supplies stored at the fort. It was abandoned in 1867. After extensive archaeological study, the post was rebuilt and is now part of the National Park Service.

Fort Wadsworth (later Fort Sisseton) was built in 1864 at Coteau des Prairies, near today's Lake City, South Dakota. It protected the northern wagon road to Montana's gold fields.

Fort Zarah, Kansas, was near the Great Bend of the Arkansas River, where it turns east and then south. The Santa Fé Trail crossed nearby Walnut Creek. In 1864, after frequent Indian raids, the post was established to protect settlers and the nearby Rath Ranch trading post. The actual site was moved twice, though the moves were only a half mile upriver. In its five years of existence, it had visits by many famous people (Buffalo Bill Cody, George Armstrong Custer, Wild Bill Hickok, Kit Carson, and Sitting Bull) and several Indian raids, including one which destroyed the trading post. A temporary town sprang up, with a hotel, two saloons, a blacksmith shop, a livery stable, a general store, and a post office. The town is now a wheat field. The fort was named after Maj. H. Zarah Curtis, who was killed by Quantrill's Raiders.

CHAPTER 8
THE STAGE ROUTES

Before the railroads, conveying mail or people to the West Coast was by stage coach (or horse) or by sea. There were two sea routes from New York to San Francisco. The first took the traveler around the southern tip of South America, with the wild seas and treacherous currents off Tierra del Fuego, then thousands of miles north. The second route was via Panama, crossing the Isthmus, with its clouds of mosquitoes bearing Yellow Fever, then up the west coast.

Travel by land meant a roughly 2,000 mile trip from St. Louis, through deserts and over mountains, in bumping, bouncing stage coaches. This meant a series of isolated posts, with lodging and changes of horses. Both on the road and at these posts there was the danger, and often the reality, of sudden attacks by Indians. It is no coincidence that the station stops coincided with a chain of military posts. Especially in the bloody summer of 1864, anyone traveling without a military escort was likely to die in a painful and grisly manner. Most readers know of stage coaches from watching movies. Their relatively smooth passage is because they travel on roads prepared for camera crews or parallel to such. The jostling, heaving, thundering, crashing, jolting experience of genuine stage travel was recorded by several diarists who clambered out of the vehicle at their final stop a mass of bruises and welts and a mental state akin to today's favored diagnosis of post-traumatic stress disorder. And that's without an Indian attack.

There were two major stage coach routes, the Overland Stage and the Butterfield Stage. The Overland Stage route began at Omaha and proceeded west, following the banks of the Platte River. The first major stop was Fort Kearney. Here a second branch, coming north from Fort Leavenworth, joined the road. Continuing west, it next encountered Fort McPherson (Cottonwood Camp) near where the Platte divided.

This route followed the South Platte and near Julesburg it passed from Nebraska into northeast Colorado, with stops at Valley Station, Fort Wardwell, and Camp Collins. Here the route swung northward into what is now Wyoming, with further stations at Fort John Buford (Fort Sanders), Fort Halleck, and Fort Bridger. Forty miles after

Fort Bridger the road crossed into Utah, terminating at Salt Lake City and its adjacent Fort Douglas.

Passengers wishing to continue onward to California had a choice of routes across Nevada and the Sierra Nevada.

The Butterfield Stage took a more southerly route. Beginning in the area of Fort Leavenworth and Kansas City, it followed the Kansas River westward to Fort Riley, then Salina, and Fort Ellsworth (Fort Harker). Five major subsidiary rivers enter the Kansas, mostly from the north, but the Smoky Hill branch enters at a far west location, halfway across Kansas. Along the Smoky Hill River was a favored route, and there were stations at Fort Fletcher (Fort Hays), Monument Station, and Fort Wallace (Pond Creek). After Pond Creek, the road entered Colorado and terminated at Denver.

The Santa Fé Trail used the same route as the Butter-field Stage until it reached Fort Ellsworth; there it branched off, traveling southwest via Fort Zarah, Fort Larned, and Fort Dodge, and on by several alternate routes to the capital of New Mexico Territory. The Santa Fé was mainly a commercial trading route rather than a stage route.

CHAPTER 9
THE SIX REGIMENTS

Hundreds of Civil War regiments have been the subject of full regimental histories. In the late 1800s these were usually compiled by self-appointed veterans of their respective regiments. In recent years, the grandchildren and great-grandchildren of veterans have been the authors, while other histories have writers inspired by some locale or battle. Most regiments were raised in a specific county or township. There was unit cohesion of place, friendship, and family ties.

Not so the United States Volunteers. Each regiment contained men from many different Confederate regiments, many different locales, and many different states. A few pairs of brothers signed up together, but in general the only common thread was escape from the boredom and starvation of prison. Post-war, it is likely that the US Volunteers did not return to their home towns and boast of having served in the Yankee army. And would they have been welcome in gatherings of the increasingly popular Sons of Confederate Veterans? For all these reasons, histories of the six regiments have been close to non-existent. The only one to receive full exposition is the First Regiment, honored in the 290 pages of *Galvanized Yankees on the Upper Missouri – The Face of Loyalty*, a superbly and deeply researched product of the pen of Michèle Tucker Butts, a professor of history at Austin Peay University. In addition to the day-to-day struggles of organizing and running a regiment, she focuses on the maturation of Col. Charles A. Dimon, whose youth and dedication oft outran his lack of frontier experience. Professor Butts also makes clear the impossible task of the military. They were supposed to mediate between the Indians, who wanted to keep their land, and the settlers and scheming promoters who wanted to take it away. The latter had the advantage of friends in Congress.

(During our own years of research in the National Archives we met "Iron Eyes," a quiet intense man, long employed by many Indian tribes, to seek out and copy the many old treaties buried in the thousands of cubic feet of records. In his many years at this work, he had never, not once, found a treaty that had been honored by the whites.)

Those who have done serious research in the National Archives can appreciate the record groups Dr. Butts analyzed: papers of the secretary of the Interior; Bureau of Indian Affairs; Register of Trader's Licenses; 1st US Volunteers books, muster rolls, reports, and returns. The list goes on: all the compiled service records of all the men who joined the six US Volunteer Regiments; all the letters sent and received by the US Continental Commands 1821-1920; pension files of all the 1st Regiment of US Volunteers; and, of course, the famous "OR," formally *The War of the Rebellion: A Compilation of the Official Records of the Union and Confederate Armies*. She delved further in the records at Carlisle Barracks, the *Congressional Record*; and the libraries of Yale University, University of North Carolina, and the Nebraska State Historical Society.

In preparation for this brief survey of galvanized Virginians, the author used not only Butts' work, but also Dee Brown's *The Galvanized Yankees*, Frederick H. Dyer's *A Compendium of the War of the* Rebellion, and *The Army Register of the Volunteer Force*.

The First United States Volunteers

The armies of both North and South had manpower shortages. Death, disease, and desertion thinned the ranks. There had been limited attempts to enlist Confederate prisoners into the Union army, but these provided more problems than benefits. The first consequential effort was begun in early 1864, by the politically powerful Maj. Gen. Benjamin Butler. Using his legendary talents of pressure and persuasion, Butler nudged President Lincoln and Secretary of War Stanton to approve recruiting men at Point Lookout. On March 28, 1864, the new recruits became the First Regiment of US Volunteers. They were initially assigned to guard and garrison duty at Norfolk, Virginia. Their one combat experience was a skirmish at Elizabeth City, North Carolina. News of this event enraged Gen. U. S. Grant, who had always opposed enlisting prisoners, and on August 9, 1864, he ordered the entire regiment to Minnesota and the Missouri River forts. They were soon on the steamer *Continental* which carried them from Norfolk to New York City. There a 28-car train carried them west, with new orders: Lieut. Col. Tamblyn was to take companies A, F, G, and I to Milwaukee. Col. Dimon took the rest, via St. Louis, to Fort Rice, where they replaced the 30th Wisconsin.

As the *Effie Deans* proceeded up the Missouri, its 25-foot stern wheel churning the muddy waters, its young colonel, the 23-year old Dimon greatly exceeded his authority, in an event which shocked the men. Pvt. William C. Dowdy, who had spoken of desertion, was charged with mutiny, sentenced to die, and shot by a firing squad, all in one day.

Dimon was a mixture of the bravado and romanticism of youth, a great overestimation of his knowledge of the frontier, and a great fear of failure since he had only tenuous control over 800 former Confederate battle veterans and, in his pocket, an admonitory letter from Ben Butler that concluded with, "I reward for good service and punish for bad, with equal facility."

Thirty-four officers served with this regiment: Col. Charles A. Dimon; Lieut. Col. William Tamblyn; Major H. G. Weymouth; Captains Hooper B. Straut, William H. Bleadenhiser, Albert C. Evans, Richard W. Musgrove, Alfred

F. Fay, William B. Upton, Samuel B. Noyes, Enoch G. Adams, James C. Michie, Benjamin R. Dimon; First Lieutenants John P. Easton, Ephraim Williams, Cyrus L. Hutchins, S. G. Bullock, David B. Wilson, Henry C. Archibald, Charles H. Champney, Halsted S. Merrill, Horace S. Hutchins, William E. Bancroft, William H. Backerman; Second Lieutenants Franklin Hedge, George E. Handy, John Teske, John E. Fullerton, Edwin Young, Herman Braun, Jeremiah C. Cronan, Charles D. Thompson; and Surgeon George H. Herrick. All survived the war except First Lieutenant Benjamin S. Wilson of Company C, who died June 2, 1865. On May 26 he had been wounded by Indians near Fort Rice, receiving three arrows and additionally a dislocated hip from falling wounded from his horse. In 1880 his mother applied for a pension.

But the regiment was not yet at Fort Rice. On September 27, the boat's captain announced that the river was too low. They would have to march the remaining 272 miles, carrying all their ammunition and supplies. On the march, which brought them successively to Crow Creek Agency, Fort Sully, and Wood Lake, they suffered from exhaustion and the chill evenings which foretold of a bitter winter. Four men died of dysentery even before they reached Fort Rice. Along the march, Dimon parlayed briefly with Two Bears, a chief of the Yankton Sioux, and convinced himself that he was now an authority on Indian affairs.

The first month at their new home was spent in finishing the earth and log fort. In this brief period, five more men died: four of dysentery and one by drowning. It was obvious that there was not enough food to last the winter and the coming of the spring floods which would lift the steamboats off the sandbars. Dimon sent out hunting parties. His fantasy of having parlayed peace on the plains was shattered when Indians wounded three men and killed a fourth. Meanwhile seven more died of disease; the main culprits were dysentery, tuberculosis, and typhoid fever. Then, in late December came the howling blizzards, carrying frozen death down from the North Pole. The boys from the Sunny South had their first taste of White Death.

An event, astonishing to us today, occurred that winter. Though the men's pay would not arrive until spring, they raised among themselves $1,000 ($30,000 in today's money) for a engraved sword, which in a formal ceremony was presented to their colonel.

The spring of 1865 brought more death. Herders were pierced by Indian arrows. Scurvy meant a burial detail almost every day. The hospital steward died. The surgeon was deathly ill. Fort Sully could not provide any supplies. On April 12, 200 mounted Indians suddenly surged from the hills, killing two soldiers and taking away 36 cattle, 19 mules, and 13 horses. A few days later, 300 Indians attacked the horse herd, leaving one soldier with an arrow in his chest. Early May brought a light moment. The wild onions had just come up. The surgeon sent out a digging detail. Within days, scurvy vanished. In mid-May the steamer *Yellowstone* arrived, bringing potatoes (also valuable in treating scurvy) and took away two groups. Company B was ordered to Fort Union; Company

K was bound for Fort Berthold. Two days later the *Deer Lodge* carried away Company H, headed for Fort Benton.

As the garrison diminished, Indian attacks increased. One sudden ambush resulted in a story both tragic and inspirational. One of the licensed traders, Charles Galpin, had an Indian wife, a very well-regarded woman, known in her native Teton language as The-Eagle-Woman-That-All-Look-At. The ambush victim was Lieut. Benjamin Wilson. The sudden impact of arrows in his back, thigh, and shoulder knocked him off his horse. As the Sioux attackers prepared to scalp him, Mrs. Galpin rushed to his side, and said in Sioux that he was hers and they could not touch him. They galloped away. The arrow in his lung doomed Wilson. After a week of suffering, and as death drew near, Wilson's last request was to look upon her face. He died holding her hand.

Summer brought changes. Col. Dimon's well-intended actions towards the Indians had actually sparked a new war, with atrocities and raiding parties. He was replaced. The long-absent paymaster arrived and the men received their wages after a ten-month delay. On July 28, 1865, a massive attack by hundreds of mounted Sioux nearly destroyed Fort Rice. Only a very determined defense, plus a few howitzer shells, drove them off. There was no little irony in the origin of this new war. Dimon's naive firing of howitzer salutes at a powwow a few weeks earlier had begun a rumor that Indians had been massacred.

There were fewer disasters that summer. Soon a steamboat carried them to Fort Leavenworth, where they mustered out in late November. But what of the four companies that had been sent to Milwaukee? Their experience included long stretches of boring and peaceful weeks, followed by the bloodshed set in motion by the Sand Creek Massacre.

This historic event took place November 29, 1864, at an encampment of peaceful Cheyenne and Arapahos. The group included roughly 70 women and children. Among the dozens of adult men were many chiefs who had advocated peaceful relations with the whites. A group of Colorado volunteers, commanded by Col. John M. Chivington, attacked in the early morning, killing most of the Indians, scalping, stabbing, and mutilating their victims. Chivington is still famous for his comment justifying the killing of Indian babies: "Nits make lice." He was a Methodist preacher, rabid Indian hater, and totally unapologetic for the killing. For generations the exact events have been debated, but many accounts include such shocking details such as the Indian womens' genitals being cut off and exhibited in Denver saloons. The four companies that did not go to Fort Rice had very different adventures.

For their first year of service, Company A went to Fort Abercrombie, Company F went to Fort Wadsworth, Company G went to Fort Ripley, and Company I went to Fort Ridgely. At these posts they served safely, afflicted only with boredom of garrison duty. In July 1865 they were ordered to Fort Snelling to be mustered out, but a last-minute telegram changed their lives.

An entrepreneur, David A. Butterfield, had raised $6 million back East to establish a new, shorter stage route from

Kansas to Denver, the so-called Smoky Hill River Valley route. On September 23, 1865, Butterfield told the press that his route, with its many way stations, would be providing daily service. Nine days later the Indian attacks began. The Butterfield Overland Despatch was over before it began. Or was it? Butterfield (and events) convinced Gen. Grenville Dodge that military protection would be mutually beneficial. Col. Tamblyn's forces were ordered west. Companies F and G were to establish and garrison Fort Fletcher. Company A was to march 100 miles westward past the new Fort Fletcher and guard the area near Monument Station, and Company I was assigned to the Pond Creek station. On November 1, 1865, the four companies took the trail toward the setting sun with 108 supply wagons, each pulled by six mules. By the time the last unit reached Pond Creek, they had been attacked many times and found several stations where the workers had been tortured to death in unspeakable ways, a horror set in motion by Chivington's Sand Creek massacre. At Monument Station they encountered Butterfield's general superintendent William R. Brewster, who had brought East Coast newspaper reporters and an artist to publicize the efficiency and safety of the new route. Instead they witnessed a raid by 500 Indians and, a few days later, barely escaped with their lives when their stagecoach was the victim of another attack. The adverse publicity added to Butterfield's woes.

The intense winter of 1865-1866 stopped all stage traffic and left the Pond Creek station with only rotten beef, mildewed bread, and ever deeper snow. They abandoned the station and headed east for Monument Station, through snow that slowed the wagons and killed the mules, but Monument Station was also starving. The two units joined forces and pushed east to Fort Fletcher. They too were starving. As all hope faded, a wagon train arrived from Fort Ellsworth.

With spring, the men were ordered back to their previous posts. As the prairie warmed, new grass sprang up, millions of wildflowers bloomed, and herds of buffalo relieved the memories of snow and bitter cold, but the change brought no cheer to Butterfield. He was going broke and sold out to Ben Holladay. Life was also changing for the last of the 1st US Volunteers. In May 1866 they marched east to Fort Leavenworth, were mustered out, and resumed civilian life.

In 1865 Colonel Dimon was promoted to the rank of brevet brigadier general of volunteers for "gallant and meritorious services."

The Second United States Volunteers

This unit, recruited at Rock Island prison, got off to an inauspicious start. The men who volunteered to galvanize were moved to a separate area, to protect them from their comrades still loyal to the Confederacy. The galvanized men were still in the rags in which they had been captured, but they could not be issued clothes because they were no long prisoners and could not be issued uniforms because they had not been officially mustered. After the camp commander burned up the telegraph wires with urgent messages, the bureaucracy finally moved. Official mustering date was

October 13, 1864. They were desperately needed out West, so now events moved more swiftly.

Thirty-seven officers served with this regiment: Col. Andrew B. Caraher; Lieut. Col. Josias R. King; Maj. William F. Armstrong; Capts. Luther F. Wyman, Alfred Wrisberg, Marion F. Bishop, Thomas J. Molony, Edward H. Gaylor, John Cowgill, Benjamin Reisdorph, William E. Hayward, Gilbert G. Lowe; First Lieuts. Henry Pennington, Joseph F. Schell, Augustus R. Robinson, Ezra F. Hinds, Charles L. Hussey, George W. Ackles, Samuel Thompson, Robert S. Schuyler, Peter H. Schwartz, William G. Graham, George W. Kingsworth, Samuel Wade; Second Lieuts. Henry Bedwell, Charles Gesell, George W. Mathews, Joseph T. Reed, Washington H. Black, Elmor Chrisman, John N. Barber, George F. Devereux, Samuel F. Cameron, Thomas D. Meley; Asst. Surgeons Daniel C. McNeil, John F. Williams; and Chaplain Alpha Wright.

The regiment lost two officers. Thirty-five-year old Surgeon Frederick Seymour was assigned to duty at Salina. He requested a leave of absence in order to have a badly needed operation. The request was denied and he was invited to resign, which he did. Capt. Carter Berkeley, of Company C, died at Fort Leavenworth of "brain fever," after six months on duty.

The spring of 1865 found the companies of the 2nd US Volunteers being shuffled about like chess pieces in response to the ever-changing Indian threats. In March, Company I was sent to Salina, Company C to Fort Ellsworth, Companies

B and K to Fort Zarah, Companies E, F, and H to Fort Larned, with Companies A, D, and G going to regimental headquarters at Fort Riley. A civilian writer, noting the new arrivals, saw them as "a miserable looking, decrepit lot, rundown physically, limited to eight miles a day, as they were unable to stand a long march." Months in prison, on a miserly diet with nearly nothing in the way of protein and vitamins had taken its toll.

In April, more changes. Company I was ordered to escort wagons on the way from Salina to Fort Ellsworth. Companies F and G were ordered to the newly established Fort Dodge. In later years this would be the wild cow town of countless movies, but when the 2nd US Volunteers arrived, it was nothing but a few sod dugouts, in no way a stronghold like Fort McHenry or Fort Sumter.

In May, Company K was moved from Fort Zarah to Little Arkansas Station. In June, men of Company K were guarding a 48-wagon train, bound for Santa Fé when a sudden ambush took away 100 mules and 75 cattle. Meanwhile at Fort Dodge a few dozen men in blue were discovered, too late, to be Indians. The loss was sixty horses. Worse, just four days later, under cover of a heavy morning fog, another raid took away the remaining animals as well as two soldiers. In 1865, most captured soldiers were found scalped, with their hands and feet cut off, and their hearts missing. Diarists traveling the western trails described mile upon mile of burned wagons, scattered household goods, and rotting corpses, both white and Indian, most of them horribly mutilated. Life on the Plains seemed headed to a crescendo of savagery.

A major change was coming. Gen. Grenville Dodge was planning a massive attack on the hostile tribes of the Southwest. Company F moved from Fort Dodge to Fort Larned, to be trained in the use of mountain howitzers; Company F marched from Salina to Fort Dodge to replace Company F. But again, there was a shift in the wind. Authorities in Washington, DC, as described by the *New York Times*, concluded that such a campaign would last longer and shed more blood that the Civil War itself. The attack was cancelled and the War Department began to plan a series of peace councils. The 2nd US Volunteers were pulled from their scattered posts and assembled at Fort Riley. From there, they marched to Fort Leavenworth and, on November 7, 1865, were mustered out.

The Third United States Volunteers

This regiment was being assembled at Rock Island at the same time as the 2nd US Volunteers. The men of the 3rd were quickly put to work guarding the stage coach line from Missouri to California and rebuilding hundreds of miles of telegraph wire cut by the Indians. In the summer of 1865 the United States was not united. All road and telegraph communication had been severed. Soldiers were desperately needed and the state volunteer men wanted out. "The Civil War is over and we want to go home." The galvanized men belonged to no state; they were going west, not home. In late February they traveled by rail to Fort Leavenworth.

The next stage of their journey was no train ride. It took the men of the 3rd US Volunteers from March 11 to April 9 to march the 350 miles to Fort Kearney. The weather was terrible, the roads were bad, and the men still weak from prison starvation. They had adequate arms and ammunition, but their uniforms and camping equipment were of poor quality. On arrival they got their orders. Companies A and B stayed at Fort Kearney. Two companies were sent to each of the following: Camp Cottonwood, Julesburg, Junction, and Fort Laramie. At each post, the companies were divided into groups of twelve men, each with a non-commissioned officer. These groups were scattered at ten mile intervals along the stage route, roughly one man for each mile of road.

The westernmost location was South Pass, Wyoming (by today's roads 1,080 miles from Rock Island) where a sub-group of Company I guarded that busy route over the Rockies. This company saw more Indians and suffered more casualties than any other company of the 3rd US Volunteers. They were involved in two disasters. The first was at Platte Bridge Station, where a battle, apparently mismanaged by a Maj. Martin Anderson, resulted in Lieut. Caspar Collins and twelve men being killed and nine men severely wounded. The second, on May 18, 1865, involved fifteen men just out of the hospital, accompanied by a wagon and a civilian driver. They were headed west to rejoin their regiment. Some officer, never identified, sent them off without a single firearm. Two miles east of Elm Creek the Indians found an easy mark. They killed two men and slashed six with sabers, pillaged the wagon, and stole the mule.

(Those with a talent for the spiritual and the transpersonal might want to drive along Interstate 80 in southern Nebraska and pull off the road sixteen miles west of Kearney. There is today's Elm Creek, population 915, with grain elevators and a residential area on the north side. Drive a few blocks and there is the creek itself. Close your eyes and recreate the absolute terror of the unarmed, totally defenseless soldiers. Feel the cold chill, the dry mouth, the hopeless desperation. Now you have warfare on the Plains.)

The regiment had thirty-five officers: Col. Christopher McNally; Lieut. Col. Samuel W. Smith; Maj. Jonas M. Bundy; Capts. David Ellison, Byron M. Richmond, A. Smith Lybe, Henry Leefeldt, Fritz Rehwinkel, Charles Fisher, Thomas Kenny, Stephen H. Matthews; First Lieuts. Earl T. Campbell, Lafayette E. Campbell, William H. Bartlett, William B. Taylor, James S. Graham, Will N. Whitlock, James L. Crowley, Melvin Stone, J. DeWitt Congdon, Richard W. Montross, Edward A. Trader, Alexander Abell; Second Lieuts. William H. Woodward, Thomas Smith, Isaac Hoch, Bloomfield E. Wells, Thomas W. Eichelberger, Albert A. Ford, William Coburn, Henry P. Leland, Frank Hudson; Asst. Surgeons Charles Harstick, Charles Becker; and Chaplain Jacob G. Forman. The regiment lost two officers. Sixty-one year old Surgeon John C. Bennett was discharged on a medical certificate, after only three months of service. Diagnosis "paralysis agitans," probably Parkinson's Disease. Capt. John S. Cochrane, age 26, born in Wheeling, Virginia, had been in the Union Maryland Cavalry. Although assigned to Company A of the 3rd US Volunteers, he spent nearly all of his time on detached service in Denver as Inspector General of the cavalry and chief of cavalry in the District of the Plains. His inspection tours included Camp Fillmore and Fort Garland in Colorado Territory. In September 1865 Thomas Kealy, a recruit for the 2nd Iowa Cavalry, gave Cochrane $450 in cash to deposit in a savings bank in Davenport. It appears that he did not deposit the money. The headquarters of the US forces in Kansas ordered Cochrane to report to the commander of the 3rd US Volunteers "for explanation of this affair." A few days later Cochrane was mustered out.

With the change in policy of massive warfare being replaced with peace councils, the 3rd US Volunteers were no longer needed. They marched the hundreds of miles back to Fort Leavenworth, where on November 29, 1865, they were mustered out.

The Fourth United States Volunteers

This unit was the second one raised at Point Lookout and its record is less glorious than its predecessor. There were only enough recruits to fill six companies and the quality of the men was deemed inferior to their predecessor. Ben Butler sent them to Norfolk but as the Indian crisis deepened they were ordered west. On their way they met many returning veterans, who regaled them with tales of Indian torture and hideous death. At St. Louis, they left the train and boarded the *Mars*. Before the boat reached Sioux City, ten percent of the men had deserted. The remaining men then traveled to Fort Rice on the *Belle Peoria*, arriving July 23, 1865. Their visions of Indian attack came true only five days later, with the Battle of Fort Rice, described earlier. At dawn, every hilltop was covered by Indians, launched on the warpath by Col. Dimon's foolish firing of a howitzer at a peace parlay. Fort Rice's new commander, Lieut. Col. John Pattee, an experienced frontiersman, coolly deployed his forces, including those of the newly arrived 4th US Volunteers. He sent Company A to form a right wing and Company D to the left. The successful defense resulted in one soldier dead and four with serious arrow wounds. It may have given the 4th Regiment men some heart that Indians were not invincible.

From Fort Rice the new men were dispersed. Company C went to Fort Berthold, where they flourished under the excellent leadership of Capt. Adams Bassett. Companies E and F went to Fort Sully, one of the worst posts in the West. Drinkable water was a mile away. The rotting huts were overrun with rats and fleas. There was nearly no grazing land. All this was made worse by an outbreak of smallpox. Fort Randall was almost as bad; poor leadership compounded defective facilities. A visiting inspector, Gen. Delos Sacket, found the men of Fort Randall in filthy uniforms, with long beards, and long hair. Their attitude seemed to be, "This is a horrible part of the world. Give it back to the Indians." The general agreed with them, adding in his report, "Fort Randall should be abandoned . . . the Territory of Dakota never will be settled by the white man."

Not even by the wildest imaginings could the men of Fort Randall have envisioned the Dakota's future outpouring of wheat, soy, barley, corn, canola, oil, and gas, not to mention such strange manifestations as Mount Rushmore and Ellsworth Air Force Base, and the even stranger tribal gathering each year at Sturgis, where half a million bikers converge for rituals beyond the comprehension of the uninitiated.

The regiment had thirteen officers: Lieut. Col. Charles C. Thornton; Capts. Samuel G. Sewall. William C. Johnson, Adams Bassett; First Lieuts. Henry O. Fox, Hamer Sutcliffe, William H. Blyton, Robert K. Wilson; Second Lieuts. William M. Eaton, William H. Vose, Joseph C. Riley, Leopold O. Parker; and Surgeon Leonard F. Russell. The regiment lost one officer, Second Lieut. Martin L. Rouse. After several months service at Crow Creek Agency, he resigned for "pressing personal reasons." His widow applied for a pension in 1904.

The scattered companies of the 4th US Volunteers were called in from their posts and mustered out by companies in June and July 1866 at Fort Leavenworth.

The Fifth United States Volunteers

This regiment had a more diverse origin. Most of the recruits came from Camp Douglas, outside of Chicago, but a considerable number came from the Alton Prison, near St. Louis, and some of the Alton men had a story of double galvanizing. On the night of December 27, 1864, just before the battle of Egypt Station, Mississippi, a lone figure emerged out of the dark. He told the Union officers that 250 of the men facing them were former Union men, who had been captured, been imprisoned, and then offered a chance at galvanizing, Southern style. To paraphrase, "When they charge, don't fire. Just take them prisoner." These new prisoners were sent to Alton where they might have been shot as deserters. Gen. Grenville Dodge had other ideas; the men were recruited into the 5th and 6th US Volunteers. (More of this story in Appendix B.) The former was organized from March to May 1865 and hurried west, where they were desperately needed.

May through July 1865 the regiment was dispersed at follows: Company A to Lake Sibley on the Republican River; Companies B, E, and F escorting wagon trains out of Salina and Fort Ripley; Companies G, K, and I escorting wagon trains on the Santa Fé Trail; and Company H, whose duties took them all the way into the Territory of New Mexico.

In August, their duties were re-shuffled. Headquarters stayed at Fort Laramie. Companies A, E, and F went to Fort Halleck. Companies G and K went to Camp Wardwell and Company B went to Denver for quartermaster duties, far from any Indians, but close to saloons and gambling. The Spring of 1866 found yet another pattern. Companies A and E went to Fort Kearney. Companies H and K went to Fort Lyon to deal with a new Indian uprising. Company G was at Fort McPherson and Company F was at Fort Collins. Companies C and D had been engaged in a far different saga. Not just arduous travel and danger but of the composition of the two companies themselves. They had both been recruited at Alton. Their backgrounds: ninety were former US soldiers, the doubly-galvanized, and sixty-nine had been Confederates who galvanized only once. The foreign-born members had origins in ten different countries. In many ways, the men resembled the French Foreign Legion.

These two companies were assigned to escort the Sawyer Wagon Road Project, a scheme which seemed to border on madness. James A. Sawyer, a businessman of Sioux City, Iowa, was a consummate promoter, booster, and schemer. He had persuaded the Federal government to give him a considerable sum of money to build a wagon road from his hometown to "the gold fields of Montana." There were many such gold fields. One major concentration was in Granite County. A computer mapping website shows that a trip by car from Sioux City to Philipsburg, a major town in Granite County, is 1,080 miles. The route traverses the entire width of South Dakota, filled in 1865 with hostile tribes, and across half of Montana.

Sawyer's group was composed of guides, engineers, laborers, and teamsters. With pick, shovel, and muscle, they were to build a road suitable for commercial wagon travel across hundreds of miles of rugged country, building bridges, filling ravines, and performing all the grading and leveling done today with huge machines. The army was to protect the enterprise with companies C and D, commanded by Capt. George W. Williford.

There were already problems. Sawyer was three weeks late in arriving at the starting point, a camp at the mouth of the Niobrara River. Three weeks' rations were consumed before the first steps on the long journey. Mature mules were unavailable, so the wagons were pulled by young mules, not up to the task. Williford was not provided with replacement shoes or uniforms; midway through the trek his men were barefoot and in rags. Worse, in moments of crisis, Williford and Sawyer fought over command and control. Their travails would fill a book, but a few high points will convey the essence of this venture.

On May 15, Companies C and D reached the mouth of the Niobrara but the expedition did not actually move until June 13. Within two weeks of travel the young mules began to give out. The first three days of July took them through the Sand Hills. The thermometer registered 106 degrees and cattle began to drop dead. On the Fourth of July they reached water and grass, but eight days later came their first Indian attack. A week later, a teamster was killed and scalped. August 14 and 15 saw massive attacks by Cheyenne, led by George Bent, son of William Bent and a Cheyenne wife. George had survived the Sand Creek massacre and vowed to kill all white soldiers. Dent demanded goods for safe passage. Williford refused but, after a bitter quarrel, Sawyers gave Bent 3,000 pounds of food and gunpowder. During the exchange one solder deserted and another was shot full of arrows. A few days later Companies C and D were ordered to nearby Fort Reno. Against all advice, Sawyers pressed on but had to be rescued from the Bad Lands near Powder River. Williford and his men spent a dreadful winter at Fort Reno, with deaths from scurvy and lung disease, Williford, too sick for duty, was ordered to Fort Casper, where he died.

At the time of mustering out, the regiment had twenty-one officers: Col. Henry E. Maynadier; Capts. George M. Bailey, Frederick Laycock, Samuel E. Mackey, Joseph M. Tomlinson, John S. Cochrane, William Hoelcke; First Lieuts. James E. Meginn, Robert E. Jones, James M. Marshall, Henry P. Humphreys, Thomas Hughes, Frederick Hubert; Second Lieuts. Howard Williams, Daniel M. Dana, William M. Harshberger, Michael McCann, A. O. Ingalls; Surgeon William C. Finlaw; and Asst. Surgeons Henry J. Smith, John D. Riddler. Sixteen officers had already departed, being either resigned, discharged honorably, or dropped from the rolls. Two officers died: Williston from heart disease and exhaustion and Second Lieut. A. Covell Dutcher who died in Denver after being shot, in circumstances not recorded in his CMSR. Capt. Randall G. Butler and First Lieut. George F. Claypoole were both dishonorably dismissed in February 1866. Butler for trading a government mule for a bay mare and stating that the horse was his personal property and Claypoole for selling government stores and keeping the money.

The regiment was mustered out by companies in October and November 1866. Col. Maynadier, a West Point man, was brevetted a brigadier general of volunteers for gallant and meritorious service for commanding the mortar fleet at Island No. 10, and major general of volunteers "while operating against hostile Indians and accomplishing much toward bringing peace with hostile tribes."

The Sixth Regiment of United States Volunteers

The men of the Sixth went further west than any other galvanized unit. When a small contingent arrived at the suburbs of Salt Lake City, they were not only unique, but cut a fine figure, being described as "splendid looking . . . intelligent and disciplined." Their comrades were further east, strung out along 500 miles of trail between Utah and Fort Kearney in Nebraska Territory. Company E protected the trail between Muddy Creek and Big Sandy. Companies A, F, and G were at Fort Laramie. Companies H and I were at Julesburg and Company K was at Cottonwood. Company B was at Camp Wardwell, and the remainder, C and D were kept at Fort Kearney.

The assembling of this regiment followed a somewhat different pattern. Six of its companies were already at Camp Douglas; two companies each, from Camp Chase and Camp Morton, joined them at Douglas. (A few of them had been the doubly-galvanized men of Egypt Station.) There, under Col. Carroll H. Potter, they were drilled, disciplined, and armed, ready to go west as a coherent unit. They went by rail from

Chicago to Fort Leavenworth, then marched two weeks to Fort Kearney. By mid-June they were dispersed to their respective posts and Col. Potter reported that all was quiet along the trail. But not for long.

June 30, 1865, at Rock Creek, Indians killed one soldier and stole sixty horses. On the Fourth of July an attack at Camp Halleck took the fourteen best stage horses. At Willow Springs, raiders took all the stock. On July 6, near Camp Wardwell, a wagon train was under attack. In September Indians were cutting telegraph lines between Fort Laramie and Caspar. Company H went to guard the section between Caspar and Sweetwater; Company I covered Fort Laramie to Caspar. In November Company B went to guard the dangerous run from Plum Creek to Julesburg, while Company E rushed to save the pontoon bridge over the Loup River. Company K was assigned to join a disastrous and ill-advised mid-winter march which ended in a mutiny and an attempt to assassinate the commander, Lieut. Col. R. H. Brown of the 12th Missouri Cavalry.

During the harsh winter of 1865-1866 some men were in no danger. Companies A, D, and F were at the other Camp Douglas near Salt Lake City, where the only conflicts were between the Mormons and the Federal government, which despised each other. Camp Douglas had manicured lawns, band concerts, and regular pay.

The 6th US Volunteers had twenty-four officers at the time of mustering out: Col. Carroll H. Potter; Lieut. Col. W. Willard Smith; Maj. Henry Norton; Capts. David I. Ezekial,

Edgar N. Sweet, Charles W. Ferrers, Carl Kostmann, Charles W. Griffith, James Sawyer; First Lieuts. Cye E. Lowes, Robert E. Flood, George K. Jenkins, Albert H. Bruman, John H. Roberts, George M. Gaylord, Hosea W. Alexander; Second Lieuts. William H. Parker, George Carlile, Stephen W. Porter, James V. Griffin, Charles Strong; Surgeon Gilbert B. Lester; and Asst. Surgeon Julius Wenz. The regiment lost two officers. First Lieut. Jacob Roesener resigned, for "pressing private reasons." Second Lieut. George F. Benson was cashiered in December 1865 at Salt Lake City for being drunk while Officer of the Day. One witness says he was drunk in bed with an enlisted man. Other witnesses disagreed.

The year 1866 brought new assignments. In April, Company F went to Fort Bridger, in the southwest corner of Wyoming. This lovely green valley offered deer, elk, sage hens, and whiskey, and little danger from Indians. In May, Company B hurried from Post Alkali to Fort Wallace; the Cheyenne had been terrorizing the stage runs. That same month Company E went to guard the Julesburg to Fort Laramie mail run. June found Company A at Fort Halleck, which was quickly abandoned in favor in building the new Fort John Buford, later Fort Sanders.

In September, Maj. Gen. William T. Sherman toured the forts of the west. He wanted all posts manned by regular army troops and ordered the US Volunteers mustered out. They completed their Federal service in October and November 1866.

CHAPTER 10
THE ROSTER

Absher, William. 64th Va. Mtd. Inf. Enrolled at Camp Lane September 1861. Corporal. Captured at Cumberland Gap September 1863. POW at Camp Douglas. Age 24. Blue eyes. 6'1". Cos. G & A, 5th US Vols. Promoted to corporal May 1866. Mostly at Fort Riley. Mustered out at Fort Kearney October 1866.

Acree (Acker), George C. 19th Va. Cav. POW September 1864 at Rock Island. Hazel eyes. 6'0". Co. B, 2nd US Vols. Promoted to Sergeant March 1865. June 1865 wagonmaster. July-August 1865 QM department. September 1865 Forage master. Mustered out

November 1865 at Forth Leavenworth, owing for lost percussion cap pouch and screwdriver.

Adams, Henry R. 37th Va. Inf. Absent sick April 1862. Absent June 1862, fell behind on the march. POW June 1862, Middleburg, Va. Exchanged August 1862. POW Cashtown, Pa. To Point Lookout via Forts McHenry and Delaware. Age 21. Hazel eyes. 6'0". Co. G, 1st US Vols. Promoted corporal September 1864. June 1864 duty at Portsmouth Ferry, Va. Mustered out at Fort Leavenworth May 1866. Invalid pension app. Died March 1909, Rush, Ky.

Adams, Samuel H. (A.) 28th Va. Inf. Absent sick with typhoid May 1861. Absent sick with diarrhea August 1862. Deserted to enemy May 1864. June 1864 at Point Lookout. Age 21. Hazel eyes. 6'0". Had been vaccinated. Co. B, 1st US Vols. October 1864-February 1865 confined to guardhouse. February 1865 court-martial. July 1865 returned to duty. September 1865 sick at Fort Rice, sent to hospital at Sioux City, from whence he was mustered out November 1865. Invalid pension app 1882. *In May 1865 Company B was en route to Fort Union and the men were shooting buffalos. Adams was locked up and missed it.*

Adcock, Roland T. Co. K, 45th Va. Inf. Enlisted May 1861. Wytheville. Drummer. POW at Camp Morton. Age 33. Blue eyes. 5'7". Co. C, 6th US Vols. Deserted on the march from Fort Leavenworth to Fort Kearney May

1865. Never paid. Never caught. Born in Granville County, N.C.

Adkins, Perry G. Co. B. 34th Bn. Va. Cav. (Musician). Captured October 1863. Age 28. Gray eyes. 5'6". Joined USV October 1864 at Rock Island. Co. E, 3rd US Vols. Mustered out at Fort Leavenworth November 1865. Invalid pension app 1881. Minor app 1917.

Ailstock (Allstock), Jordan D. Co. G. 11th Va. Cav. Born Rockbridge County. Captured Madison Courthouse, September 22, 1863. Sent to Point Lookout via Old Capitol Prison. Age 32. Gray eyes. 5'10". Had been vaccinated. Co. E, 1st US Vols. May 1864 guarding Portsmouth Ferry Boat Landing. Died of typhoid at Fort Rice September 1865. Some issue of $70 in "notes" in Personal Effects. Buried Custer Battlefield National Military Cemetery, site 402. Lucinda widow app 1880.

Akers, Andrew H. (Anderson Akers). 63rd (McMahon's) Va. Inf. Captured May 1864 at Dallas, Ga. POW at Rock Island. Age 18. Hazel eyes. 5' 10". Co. E, 2nd US Vols. Mustered out at Fort Leavenworth November 1865. An Anderson Akers served in the 1850 Indian Wars, Bagby's Company, Texas Mounted Volunteers.

Aleshire, David F. (Frank Ailshire).10th Va. Inf. Vols. Blacksmith. Had pneumonia 1862. Born Page, Va. POW at Point Lookout. Age 19. Gray eyes. 5'6". Co. H. 1st US Vols. Died of scurvy April 3, 1865 at Fort Rice. Buried Custer Battlefield National Cemetery, site 344.

Allen, Perry. 34th Bn.Va. Cav. (Also in David S. Hounshell's Bn.) POW at Point Lookout. Age 22. Blue eyes. 6'0". Co. C. 4th US Vols. Enlisted October 1864. November 1864 company cook in 2nd US Vols. Orderly in medical dept. June-November 1865. Duty at post hospital December 1865-May 1866. Mustered out at Fort Leavenworth July 1866. Invalid pension app 1892. Widow pension app 1914.

Alley, Ballard P. (Richard Allie). 63rd (McMahon's) Va. Inf. Deserted and POW July 1864 at Chattahoochee River, Ga. POW at Camp Morton. Age 25. Blue eyes. 5'9". Co. G, 6th US Vols. April 1866 company clerk. September 1866 made corporal. Mustered out at Fort Kearney October 1866. Lived in California postwar. Invalid pension app 1905.

Anderson, Samuel A. Co. A (other sources say Co. C), 43rd Virginia Cavalry Battalion (Mosby's Regiment). Captured May 5, 1863 at Union Mills in Fairfax County. POW at Old Capitol, then Fort McHenry, then Fort Delaware, finally Point Lookout. Age 16. Gray eyes. 5'6". Had diarrhea 1863. Had been vaccinated. Took Oath of Allegiance June 9, 1864 and galvanized. Co. G, 1st US Vols. October 1864 at Northern Stockade Line. January-June 1865 orderly duty at District HQ, St. Paul. Deserted at Fort Snelling September 1865, taking his tent, canteen, and knapsack. Issued a discharge in 1925.

Anderson, William Henry. 11th Va. Cav. (enlisted Bath County, Va.). Saber wound and POW Orange County, Va. August 1862. Exchanged. POW Sept. 1863, Madison County, Va. To Point Lookout via Old Capitol Prison. Did not want to be exchanged. Age 30. Gray eyes. 5'10". Not vaccinated. Illiterate. Enlisted February 1864. Co. A then E, 1st US Vols. December 1864-June 1865 wheelwright at Fort Abercrombie. September 1865 promoted to corporal. December 1865 post carpenter at Monument Station, Ks. February 1866 building quarters. Mustered out at Fort Leavenworth May 1866. Died 1900. Buried Mt. Pleasant Cemetery, Covington, Va.

Andrews, William. 50th Va. Inf. (45th Va. Inf. ?). POW at Point Lookout. Age 19. Blue eyes. 5'9". Freckles. Illiterate. Had been vaccinated. Typhoid fever 1863. Co. H, 1st US Vols. October 1865 guarding wagon train from Fort Rice to Fort Leavenworth, where he was mustered out November 1865. 1898 invalid pension app. 1916 widow app.

Arbigast (Arbogast), Ephriam. 25th (Heck's) Va. Inf. Hospitalized August 1863 with abscess. POW May 1864 at Mine Run, Va. At Point Lookout via Belle Plain. Age 21. Blue eyes. 5'11". Had been vaccinated. Drinks but never had the "horrors" (DTs). Co. K, 1st US Vols. On detached service from Fort Rice to Fort Leavenworth October 1865. Mustered out at Fort Leavenworth November 1865.

Ayers (Aryes), Jefferson. 17th Va. Cav. Deserted July 1863. POW at Rock Island. Age 29. Dark eyes. 5'8". Co. H, 2nd US Vols. April 1865 reduced to private from corporal. April 1865 in hospital at Fort Larned. May-September in hospital at Fort Riley with ulcers of both corneas. Medical discharge October 1865. Died July 1887, Wirt County, W.Va. Widow app 1890.

Bailey, Henry C. Co. B, 48th Va. Inf. POW at Camp Douglas. Age 25. Blue eyes. 5'5". Illiterate. Co. G, 5th US Vols. June 1865 deserted at Cottonwood Crossing, taking all his equipment. Never caught.

Bailey, William L. 37th Va. Inf. POW at Point Lookout. Age 23. Blue eyes. 5'5". Illiterate. Had been vaccinated. Co. C, 1st US Vols. August 1865 at Fort Rice. September 1865 in hospital at St. Louis. October 1865 mustered out sick at Sioux City.

Bain, William. 13th Va. Cav. POW at Point Lookout. Age 22. Blue eyes. 5'9". Illiterate. Co. B, 4th US Vols. Mustered out as 1st Sgt. at Fort Leavenworth, Ks. June 1866. 1887 requests replacement discharge. Invalid pension app 1892.

Baird, William. 41st (White's) Bn. Va. Cav. POW at Rock Island. Age 31. Gray eyes. 5'8". Illiterate. b. Scotland. Co. E, 2nd US Vols. May 1865 on escort duty to Fort Larned. Mustered out at Fort Leavenworth November 1865.

Baker, Noah. 64th Va. Mtd. Inf. POW at Camp Douglas. Age 21. Hazel eyes. 5'7". Illiterate. Co. H, 5th US Vols. June

1865 owed $2.50 to sutler at Fort Riley. July 1865 escorting wagons to Fort Lyon. November 1865 deserted at Fort Kearney, taking knapsack, haversack, tent, canteen, and bugle badge. Never caught. (There is an 1891 pension app. for a Noah Baker of the "5th US Inf.")

Baumgardner (Bumgardner), James A. 63rd (McMahon's) Va. Inf. POW at Rock Island. Age 22. Dark eyes. 5'6". Co. A, 3rd US Vols. June 1865 on detached service "guarding M. station, C.M.L.R." (O.M.L.R.?) Mustered out as private at Fort Leavenworth November 1865. Charged $2.90 for damage to property of John Mattis (post sutler?).

Bell, Benjamin G. 64th Va. Inf. POW at Point Lookout. Age 20. Hazel eyes. 5'7". Had been vaccinated. Co. I, 1st US Vols. Assigned to QM Dept. November 1864 and March-April 1865. June 1865 absent sick at Fort Snelling, where he was mustered out as private, owing for a "destroyed bed sack, haversack, and canteen."

Bell, Charles A. 49th Va. Inf. POW at Point Lookout. Age 27. Blue eyes. 5'9". He had been vaccinated. He had typhoid in 1862 and smallpox in 1863. Co. B, 1st US Vols. He deserted at St. Louis, and was captured at Sioux City. He was returned to duty without trial "in accordance with War Dept. instructions." He was at Fort Rice in March 1865 and was mustered out at Fort Leavenworth November 1865, owing $19.60 for clothing. The charges were removed in 1869.

Benson, John G. 25th (Heck's) Va. Inf. POW at Point Lookout. Age 20. Blue eyes. 5'6". Had been vaccinated. In CSA had a fractured left clavicle. Co. H, 1st US Vols. Died in Fort Rice post hospital April 21, 1865 of scurvy. Remains removed to site 403 Custer National Military Cemetery.

Blankenship (Blackenship), Joseph T. 25th Bn. Va. Inf. (Also served in 44th Va. Inf. and 20th Bn. Va. Heavy Artillery.) POW at Point Lookout. Age 20. Hazel eyes. 6'4". Co. A, 4th US Vols. Convicted by court-martial of Article 23 (advising desertion) and given a year in prison. There his behavior was so good (great prose) that his sentence was soon remitted. In April 1866 he was an attendant at the Fort Leavenworth hospital. He was mustered out at Fort Leavenworth June 1866. Invalid pension app 1890. Living in Appomattox County 1870 and Chesterfield County 1930, with his 49-year old son. d. 1943 at Petersburg, Va. (Wife Martha 1844-1929).

Blevins, Andrew. 63rd (McMahon's) Va. Inf. POW Rock Island. Age 21. Blue eyes. 6'1". Illiterate. Co. H, 2nd US Vols. April-June 1865 battery duty Fort Zarah, then Fort Larned. Mustered out at Fort Leavenworth November 1865. Invalid pension app 1892.

Bowles, George W. 30th Bn. Va. S.S. POW at Point Lookout. Age 21. Blue eyes. 5'8". Illiterate. Co. B, 4th US Vols. (created from 2nd US Vols.?) February 1865 detached service, no details. November 1865 special duty.

December 1865 police duty. March-April 1866 QM duty. Mustered out at Fort Leavenworth June 1866. Invalid pension app 1892. Widow app undated.

Boyd, Asa E. 42nd Va. Inf. POW at Point Lookout. Age 21. Gray eyes. 5'11". Had been vaccinated. 1862 abscess of thigh. "Arm dislocated seven years ago." Piles "sometimes." Co. A, 1st US Vols. Mustered out at Fort Leavenworth May 1866.

Bradley, Phillip (John). 24th Va. Cav. POW at Point Lookout. Age 28. Blue eyes. 5'0". Had been vaccinated. b. N. Ireland. Occupation caulker. Typhoid 1859. Drinking history? "Sometimes." Co. A, 1st US Vols. In Milwaukee jail drunk July 1864. Deserted at Milwaukee August 1864, taking knapsack and bugle badge. Never caught.

Bray, John T. 50th Va. Inf. POW at Point Lookout. Age 25. Blue eyes. 5'11". Had been vaccinated. Typhoid in CSA. Co. D, 1st US Vols. Deserted August 1864 at Norfolk, taking his musket. Invalid pension app 1901.

Bray, Michael D. 64th Va. Mtd. Inf. POW at Camp Douglas. Age 22. Brown eyes. 5'4". Co. H, 5th US Vols. April 1865 in hospital at Fort Dodge. June 1865 at Fort Riley. October 1865 on detached service at "Buffalo Station." Owed 16 cents for lost tampions. Mustered out at Fort Leavenworth November 1866. Invalid pension app 1901.

Broden, John William. 6th Va. Cav. b. May 16, 1830 in Fauquier Co. Signed enlistment with "X." POW at Point Lookout. Age 30. Gray eyes. 5'6". Had been vaccinated. Had measles 1850. Co. B, 1st US Vols. December 1864 three month's service with mounted infantry. Mustered out at Fort Leavenworth November 1865. Charged two cents for lost tampion. Invalid pension app 1908. Widow app 1915 at Harrisonburg Va. Married Fannie Deeds 1854. Married Rebecca Fultz 1873. He died November 28, 1914. Buried Mabel Memorial Chapel, Route 6, Harrisonburg. (Michael P. Musick, *6th Virginia Cavalry*, 1990, p. 99.)

Brown, Baswell (Bazwell). 50th Va. Inf. POW at Point Lookout. Age 45. Blue eyes. 5'8". Had been vaccinated. Illiterate. In CSA, had "fever" and "piles." Co. I, 1st US Vols. Mustered out at Fort Leavenworth May 1866.

Brown, Horace. 12th Bn. Va. Lt. Arty. b. in Galveston. POW at Camp Douglas. Age 45. Blue eyes. 5'8". Had been vaccinated. Co. E, 6th US Vols. Deserted after six months service. In jail at Fort Leavenworth, charged with inducing men to desert, form a guerilla band, and head south, living by robbery. At Fort Kearney he escaped and was never recaptured. Invalid pension app 1872. (He does not match with CSA records. Horace Nimrod Brown served with Sturdivant's Battery {12th Bn. Va. Light Artillery, Co. A,} and was present in Confederate service the entire war, paroled at Charlottesville in May 1865.)

Buntrum (Brenter, Bundrant), William H. 42nd Va. Inf. POW at Point Lookout. Age 22. Blue eyes. 5'9". Illiterate. Co. E, 4th US Vols. QM duty November 1865 to May 1866.

Mustered out at Fort Leavenworth. Invalid pension app 1890. Widow app 1919.

Butler, Andrew J. 41st Va. Inf. POW at Point Lookout. Age 21. Light blue eyes. 5'9". Had been vaccinated. He had enlisted in the 41st Va, Inf. May 29, 1861, an illiterate from Hanover County. He spent January through April 1863 in Richmond General Hospital with pneumonia, went AWOL and deserted to the Union. Co. K, 1st US Vols. Many months sick in hospital at Portsmouth and St. Louis, Mo. AWOL en route from Baltimore to Columbus, Oh. February 1865 court-martialed (RG153, OO691) at Fort Ripley, Mn. He had left his sentry post and gone in the hay shed. (Probably freezing.) File contains a map and note of "good character." At mustering out, he was absent, owing the government for clothes and an Enfield rifle.

Byrd, Thomas W. 11th Va. Cav. POW at Point Lookout. Age 20. Blue eyes. 5'8". Co. C, 1st US Vols. Deserted September 1865 at Fort Rice. Captured at Fort Sully. Owed for $101 in QM stores and $40 in ordnance. Restored to duty without trial in G.O. 136. Mustered out November 1865 Fort Leavenworth.

Caldwell, John F. 5th Va. Inf. Captured near Atlanta July 1864. POW at Camp Douglas. Age 23. Blue eyes. 5'9". Co. F, 6th US Vols. April 1865 sentry at guard house. March 1865 lost haversack. Owed 65 cents. October 1865 on QM duty. August 1866 company cook. Mustered out

October 1866. Invalid pension app 1887. Widow app 1905.

Campbell, John A. 31st Va. Inf. POW at Point Lookout. Age 20. Hazel eyes. 5'8". Co. A, 4th US Vols. Mustered out Fort Leavenworth June 1866. Invalid pension app. 1911.

Cayson (Cason), John W. 16th Va. Inf. POW Point Lookout. Age 23. Dark eyes. 5'11" Had been vaccinated. Had "Porrigo" (ringworm) of scalp. Enlisted February 1864. Co. F, 1st US Vols. On picket at Zion's Church. Duty at Ponts Ferry, Norfolk. February 1865 detailed as teamster. November 1865 escorting train from Fort Fletcher to Monument Station, Ks. April 1866 QM duty at Fort Fletcher. Mustered out May 1866 at Fort Leavenworth. Widow app 1891.

Chaney, William T. (or P). 22nd Va. Cav. (Bowen's Regt.) POW at Rock Island. Age 26. Blue eyes. 5'9". Co. D, 2nd US Vols. March through September 1865 provost guard duty at Leavenworth City, Ks. Mustered out at Fort Leavenworth November 1865. Invalid pension app 1886.

Cheek, Isaiah. 50th Va. Inf. POW at Point Lookout. Age 20. Blue eyes. 5'10". Illiterate. Had "fever" in CSA. Had been vaccinated. Co. I, 1st US Vols. QM duty October 1864, May-June 1865, and October 1865. November 1865 teamster on wagon train to Fort Lyon. January 1866 company cook. April 1866 teamster duty. June 1865 owed $2.10 for broken Enfield bayonet. Mustered out

August 1866 at Fort Leavenworth. Invalid pension app 1890. Widow app 1921.

Cofer, James E. 42nd Va. Inf. POW at Point Lookout. Age 18. Blue eyes. 6'1". Had been vaccinated. Had "fever" in CSA service. Co. K, 1st US Vols. July 1864 provost guard Norfolk Va. September 1865 hay guard. Possibly at Fort Berthold. Owed 61 cents for lost "C & B Equip." Promoted to Sergeant. Mustered out at Fort Leavenworth November 1865.

Colley, William. Co. B, 48th Va. Inf. Captured at Spotsylvania CH May 1864. POW at Point Lookout. Age 18. Hazel eyes. 5'8". Had been vaccinated. Pre-war was a boatman. Co. H, 1st US Vols. Promoted to Corporal. Sick at Fort Rice September 1865. Sent down river to hospital at Sioux City, then to hospital in St. Louis. Discharged "convalescent" October 1865.

Collins, Daniel M. 2nd and 4th Va. Inf. Wounded September 1862. Captured at Spotsylvania CH May 1864. POW at Point Lookout. Age 23. Blue eyes. 6'1". Had been vaccinated. Illiterate. Cataract left eye. Co. A, 1st US Vols. December 1865 on escort duty to Fort Ellsworth. Mustered out at Fort Leavenworth May 1866. Invalid pension app 1883. Widow app undated.

Collins, Daniel. Co. A, 62nd Va. Mtd. Inf. Captured at Baxter Co. POW at Point Lookout (other records say Rock Island). Age 38. Gray eyes. 5'11". Illiterate. Co. B, 3rd US Vols. Sick in hospital at Fort Kearney March-May 1865. June-October 1865 QM duty. Mustered out at Fort

Leavenworth November 1865. Invalid pension app 1888. Widow undated.

Collins, John C. (P.) 1st Bn. Va. Inf. (Irish Bn.). POW at Point Lookout. Age 18. Blue eyes. 5'5". b. Dublin, Ireland. Illiterate. Had been vaccinated. Co, A. 1st US Vols. Deserted on the march August 1865 from Fort Abercrombie to Sauk Center and Fort Snelling, taking bed sack, scales, bugle badge, haversack, and knapsack. November 1865 re-joined unit. December 1865 in confinement at Fort Fletcher. March 1866 company cook. Mustered out at Fort Leavenworth May 1866.

Collins, John W. Co. H, 45th Va. Inf. Captured at Winchester September 1864. POW at Point Lookout. Co. D, 4th US Vols. Invalid pension app 1890. Widow app 1908.

Collins, Richard Jasper (Joseph R. Collins). 50th Va. Inf. POW at Point Lookout. Age 25. Gray eyes. 5'11". Illiterate. Chronic diarrhea 1863. Never been vaccinated. Co. H, 1st US Vols. Sick in Union hospitals with chronic diarrhea: Norfolk June 1864; August 1864 through April 1865 at St. Louis; October 1865 at Sioux City and St. Louis. On duty one month at Fort Rice before being sent "down river" for sickness.

Colton, William. 48th Va. Inf. POW at Point Lookout. Age 25. Hazel eyes. 6'0". Illiterate. Had pneumonia 1863. Also "wounded by a blow from a stick." Had been vaccinated. Co. H, 1st US Vols. Deserted at St. Louis August 1864. Never caught. Owed $25.46 for gun, knapsack and canteen.

Conner, James A. Capt. Archibald Graham's Co.; 1st Co. Virginia Rockbridge Light Artillery. 18-years old when enlisted April 1861 as a wagoner. Wounded at Sharpsburg September 1862. Wounded at Gettysburg July 1863. Captured at Waterloo, Pa. (About 20 miles north of Chambersburg) July 1863. POW at Point Lookout. Age 29. Gray eyes. 5'8". Had been vaccinated. Co. E, 1st US Vols. "Served in Northwest Territory." Deserted at Fort Rice September 1865. He owed $155.65 for stolen QM property. Soon captured. Returned to duty without trial in response to G.O. 136. Mustered out November 1865. All charges dropped 1888. Invalid pension app 1888. Died January 21, 1903. Widow app undated.

Cook, Mathew E. Co. G. 22nd Va. Inf. Captured at Winchester September 1864. POW at Point Lookout. Co. A, 4th US Vols. Minor pension app 1882. Widow app 1925.

Cooley, George W. (or A). Co. A, 37th Va. Inf. POW at Rock Island. Age 24. Wheelwright. Blue eyes. 5'8". Co. H, 3rd US Vols. June 1865 on detached service at "Beaver Creek station." July 1865 company cook. Mustered out at Fort Leavenworth November 1865.

Cooper, William. Co. A, 47th Va. Inf. Enlisted May 1861. Wounded at Gettysburg July 1863. Captured November 1863 at Mine Run. POW at Point Lookout. 5' 9". Blue eyes. Dark hair. Co. E, 1st US Vols. Died October 1865 at Fort Rice "from the effects of poison."

Cordell, Abner. Co. K, 63rd (McMahon's) Va. Inf. Captured November 1863 at Missionary Ridge, Tn. POW at Rock Island. Age 40. Gray eyes. 5'7". Illiterate. Co. B, 2nd US Vols. May 1865 on escort to Cow Creek, Ks. Mustered out as a private at Fort Leavenworth November 1865.

Cox, Charles F. Co. A, 52nd Va. Inf. 18-year old carpenter's apprentice. Court-martialed February 1863 for AWOL. Captured September 1864 at Fisher's Hill. POW at Point Lookout. Age 24. Wheelwright. Blue eyes. 5'8". Co. D, 4th US Vols. In hospital at Norfolk, Va. February 1865, wounded. July 1865 carpenter with QM. Mustered out at Fort Leavenworth June 1866. Invalid pension app 1888. d. March 1926 at Hot Springs, S.D., probably at the Battle Mountain Veterans Sanitarium.

Cumby, John (James, J.J.) Co. I, 42nd Va. Inf. Deserted September 1862 at Antietam. AWOL July 1863. Captured at Wilderness May 1864. POW at Point Lookout. Age 26. Blue eyes. 5'8" Had been vaccinated. Had "rheumatism." Illiterate. Co. E, 1st US Vols. In May 1865 was wounded by Indians while on outpost near Fort Rice. Gunshot wound of middle third of right radius and ankylosis of right elbow. In hospital at St. Louis until September 1865 when he received a medical discharge. Invalid pension app 1869. Undated widow app.

Cundiff, John T. 55th Va. Inf. Missing since Battle of Falling Waters July 14, 1863. POW at Point Lookout. Had been vaccinated. Had pneumonia 1858. Age 19. Blue eyes.

5'4". Mariner. Co. F, 1st US Vols. May 1865 guarding hay train. November 1865 escorting train from Fort Fletcher to Monument Station, Ks. December 1865 log detail. February 1866 working on quarters at Fort Fletcher. May 1866 on QM duty. Mustered out as private at Fort Leavenworth May 1866.

Davidson, Joseph E. Co. C, 64th Va. Mtd. Inf. Enlisted September 1861. No record of sickness while in Confederate service. Captured at Cumberland Gap September 9, 1863. POW at Camp Douglas. Age 23. Gray eyes. 5'6". Illiterate. Co. K, 6th US Vols. Mustered in April 3, 1865. May through July 1865 sick in hospital at Fort Leavenworth. Discharged (medically) August 1865. Invalid pension app 1890.

Davidson, Martin V. Co. C, 45th Va. Inf. POW at Point Lookout. Age 21. Blue eyes. 5'7". Co. D, 4th US Vols. September and October 1865 sick in hospital at Sioux City, Ia. Discharged "convalescent" November 1865. Unit mustered out June 1866. Widow app 1883.

Davidson, Wayne D. 64th Va. Mtd. Inf. Captured at Cumberland Gap September 9, 1863. POW at Camp Douglas. Mustered in April 3, 1865. (Probably brother of Joseph E. Davidson). Age 21. Gray eyes. 5'11". Co. C, 6th US Vols. June 1865 company cook. July 1865 teamster. August and September 1865 at Bishop Ranch N.T. October 1865 deserted from Fort Cottonwood, N.T., taking $111.23 of government equipment. Never caught.

Davis, Peter. Co. C, 26th Va. Inf. Enlisted February 1862 at age 17. Wounded and captured at Webb's Farm June 1864. POW at Point Lookout. Age 20. Blue eyes. 5'6". Illiterate .Co. C (D). 4th US Vols. (which had been the 2nd US Vols). On duty as company wagoner November 1865 through May 1866. Mustered out at Fort Leavenworth July 1866.

Davis, Samuel. Co. C, 1st Va. Cav. "Deserted to US Forces." (There were two Samuel Davises in the US Vols.)

Davis, Samuel. POW at Rock Island. Age 25. Brown eyes. 5'7". (Next page of CMSR says age 23, 5'9".) Illiterate. Co. E, 2nd US Vols. Mustered out at Fort Leavenworth November 1865.

Davis, Samuel. POW at Camp Douglas. Age 35. Gray eyes. 5'5". Illiterate. Co. G, 5th US Vols. March 1866 teamster in QM Dept. April 1866 company cook. May 1866 QM dept. July 1866 teamster. August-September company cook. Mustered out at Fort Kearney October 1866.

Delong, Samuel T. Co. E, 50th Va. Inf. Enlisted July 1861 Smyth County. POW at Fort Donelson February 1862. Exchanged at Vicksburg November 1862. Hospitalized twice in 1863. Captured May 1864 Spotsylvania CH. POW at Point Lookout. Age 23. Brown eyes. 5'7". Had been vaccinated. Co. I, 1st US Vols. October 1864 to April 1865 QM Dept. Deserted October 1865 at Fort Leavenworth, owing for NCO sword belt. Never caught. 1891 charges dismissed.

Dempsey, Patrick. Co. A, 21st (Peter's) Va. Cav. Deserted twice in 1864. Captured at Strasburg, Va. September 1864. POW at Point Lookout. Blacksmith. b. Ireland. Age 32. Gray eyes. 5'10". Enlisted in Co. B. 4th US Vols. October 1864-December 1864 company clerk. December 1865 police duty. Mustered out as Sgt. at Fort Leavenworth June 1866.

Denton, Robert M. Co. F, 49th Va. Inf. POW at Point Lookout. Age 18. Blue eyes. 5'6". Co. A, 4th US Vols. Also served in 2nd US Vols. October 1864 sick in hospital Norfolk, Va. May and June 1865 sick in hospital (anemia and dysentery) at Benton Barracks and St. Louis Marine Hospital. Convalescent discharge July 1865. Invalid pension app. 1890. d. Harrisonburg, Va. 1914. Buried in Woodbine Cemetery.

Dickey, Joseph B. 36th Bn. Va. Cav. POW at Rock Island. Age 21. Gray eyes. 5'10". Illiterate. Co. E, 2nd US Vols. May 1865 sick in hospital Fort Zarah, Ks. Mustered out at Fort Leavenworth November 1865. Invalid pension app 1890. Widow app undated.

Dixon, William M. Co. D, 64th Va. Mtd. Inf. Captured Cumberland Gap September 1863. POW at Camp Douglas. Age 21. Blue eyes. 5'10". Illiterate. Co. C, 5th US Vols. Record is confused. He was probably discharged sick May 1865 from Fort Leavenworth, while his regiment marched on.

Dollarhigher (Dollahig), Edmond (Edward) A. 45th Va. Inf. POW at Point Lookout. Age 22. Hazel eyes. 6'0".

Illiterate. Co. D, 4th US Vols. November 1864 to March 1865 company cook. November 1865 QM Dept. May 1866 Ordnance Dept. Mustered out at Fort Leavenworth June 1866.

Donahue (Donohue), James. 41st Va. Cav. POW at Rock Island. Age 22. Dark eyes. 5′6″. b. Ireland. Co. B, 2nd US Vols. April-June 1865 QM duty. July 1865 company cook. Mustered out at Fort Leavenworth November 1865.

Donovan (Donevant), James. Co. H, 44th Va. Inf. Born 1824 Cork, Ireland. Substitute for William A. Phauss. Captured at Spotsylvania CH May 1864. POW at Point Lookout. Co. H, 1st US Vols. Died of scurvy Fort Rice April 1865.

Douglas, Robert. Co. K, 1st Va. Cav. Resident of Baltimore. 5′11″ Blue eyes. Captured at Leesburg September 1863. POW at Rock Island. b. Scotland. Age 27. Light eyes. 5′10″. Co. B, 2nd US Vols. March 1865 in confinement Fort Leavenworth. May 1865 on escort to Cow Creek, Ks. Mustered in and out as Sgt. Mustered out November 1865.

Eldar (Elder), Hiram T. Co. E, 11th Va. Inf. Captured Milford Station, Va. May 1864. POW at Point Lookout. Age 22. 5′8″. Illiterate. Born Halifax, Va. Co. D, 4th US Vols. Deserted January 1865 at Norfolk, Va. Died June 13, 1907 at Brookneal, Va., his birthplace.

Embery (Embrey), Sanford E. Co. E, 7th Va. Inf. Captured at Gettysburg 1863. POW at Point Lookout. Age 27. Blue eyes. 5'9". Had typhoid in 1860. Illiterate. Had been vaccinated. Co. B, 1st US Vols. June 1864 provost duty Norfolk Va. August 1865 at Fort Union, M.T. Mustered out at Fort Leavenworth November 1865.

Enrufty (Enroughty), Madison F. Co. C, 2 1st Bn. Va. Lt. Arty. AWOL 6 months in 1862. Captured at Fort Harrison, Va. September 1864. POW at Point Lookout. Age 18. Blue eyes. 5'7". Blacksmith. Co. A, 4th US Vols. Also 2nd USV. November 1864 sick in hospital Norfolk, Va. June 1865 company cook. July-August 1865 baker. Courier at Fort Sully, D.T. September 1865 to April 1866. Mustered out at Fort Leavenworth June 1866.

Erwin, William G. Co. M, 1st US Vols. Cannot locate CMSR. Invalid pension app 1928. Served in 19th US Infantry in Spanish-American War.

Erwin, William N. Co. A, 6th Ga. Cav. Sick at Anderson Springs, Tx. October 1863. Captured at Clay County, N.C. December 10, 1863. POW at Rock Island. Age 31. Hazel eyes. 5'5". Co. A, 3rd US Vols. May-June 1865 "building govt. houses and stables O.L.M.R." July 1865 QM Dept. Mustered out Fort Leavenworth November 1865. Invalid pension app 1881. d. June 6, 1914 at Greeley, Co. Buried in Old La Veta Cemetery, La Veta, Huerfano County, Colorado. Buried with wife Rachel.

Erwin, William R. 31st Va. Inf. POW at Point Lookout. Age 21. Blue eyes. 5'11". (A man with this name was in the Seminole Wars, 2nd Tn. Mtd. Inf.) Co. A, 4th US Vols. July-August in confinement at Fort Sully. September

1865 released from arrest. September 1865-May 1866 on courier duty at Fort Sully. Owed for lost pistol cartridge box. Mustered out at Fort Leavenworth June 1866.

Fainter, James A. Co. H, 4th Va. Inf. b. November 19, 1838. 5'11". Farmer. Light complexion, dark eyes. AWOL October 1862. Wounded at Drewry's Bluff 1864. Captured at Gettysburg July 3, 1863. POW at Point Lookout. Enlisted in Co. B, 1st US Vols. on January 25, 1864. Deserted August 1864 and enlisted in Co. F, 12th New York Cavalry, apparently under the name of Alexander Hogue. Mustered out honorably from the NY regiment June 20, 1865. Applied for pension 1909. Rejection letter states, "Your above cited claim for pension under the act of Feb. 6, 1907, is rejected on the ground of no title you having deserted from Co. B, 1, U.S. Vol. Inf. And by reason of your last contract for service in Co. F, 12, N.Y. Vol. Inf. [sic] received bounty other than from the United States in excess of that to which you would have been entitled had you faithfully performed your contract for service in Co. B, 1, U.S. Vol. Inf." He had received $600 bounty for joining the NY regiment, roughly $18,000 in today's money.

Falls, William T. Co. H, 14th Va. Inf. Captured at Howlett's House, Va. August 1864. POW at Point Lookout. Age 18. Blue eyes. 5'4". Illiterate. Co. B, 4th US Vols. Mustered out at Fort Leavenworth June 1866. Invalid pension app 1877. Widow app 1921. d. December 1920 W.Va.

Farmer, Isaac. Co. D, 50th Va. Inf. September 1863 hospitalized at Richmond for fever, then a month sick leave. Captured May 1864 at Spotsylvania CH. POW at Point Lookout. Age 23. Lt. brown eyes, other records say lt. blue. 5'7". Illiterate. Had been vaccinated. Co. H, 1st US Vols. Died of scurvy February 21, 1865 Fort Rice. Reburied at Custer National Military Cemetery, site 419. Pension app by mother 1870.

Farrer (Farrar), Robert H. Co. H, 11th Va. Inf. 22-year old farmer. Wounded 1862. Captured at Gettysburg July 1863. POW at Point Lookout. Age 29. Dark eyes. 5'6". b. Ireland. Co. B, 1st US Vols. Cannot locate CMSR. Mustered out as corporal. Widow app 1883.

Farris, Caleb. Co. G, 25th Va. Cav. Captured April 1864 at Clainborne, Tn. POW at Rock Island. Age 19. Blue eyes. 5'7" (5'10"). Illiterate. Co. E, 2nd US Vols. April 1865 escort train to Fort Lyon, C.T. May 1865 escort train to Fort Larned, Ks. Mustered out at Fort Leavenworth November 1865 as corporal.

Ferguson, Benjamin. Co. G, 3rd Va. Inf. Enlisted age 17. Captured at Petersburg June 1864. POW at Point Lookout. Age 20. Gray eyes. 5'7". Co. E, 4th US Vols. May 1865 deserted from steamer *Mars* near Omaha, N.T., owing $4.94. Never caught. Died in California 1871. A Benjamin F. Ferguson died December 9, 1930 and is buried in Roosevelt Memorial Park, Gardena,

Ca. (Find-A-Grave shows a bronze marker flush with the grass and a note "member of the GAR".)

Fletcher, Jordan T. Co. D, 64th Va. Mtd. Inf. Captured at Cumberland Gap. POW at Camp Douglas. Age 25. Hazel eyes. 5'6". Illiterate. Co. G, 5th US Vols. June-September 1865 teamster. January-February 1866 company cook. March 1866 hospital orderly. April 1866 company cook. May-June 1866 QM Dept. August 1866 at Fort McPherson, N.T. Mustered out at Fort Kearney, N.T. October 1866. Invalid pension app 1890. Widow pension app 1925. d. at Cassard, Va. 1925.

Forrest, Zacharia G. Co. K, 1st Va. Cav. Captured at Berry's Ferry, Va. POW at Rock Island. Age 31. Light eyes. 5'8". Engineer. Co. B, 2nd US Vols. Mustered in and out as Sergeant. Post-war in York, Pa.

Foutz, Osborn. Co. F, 23rd Bn. Va. Inf. Captured September 1864 Winchester. POW at Point Lookout. Age 21. Brown eyes. 6'0". Co. E, 4th US Vols. From September 1864 to May 1865 he was in Balfour Hospital, Portsmouth, Va. (Eight months!) He died of chronic diarrhea May 1865.

Fox, James. Co. F, 41st Va. Cav. POW at Rock Island. Age 24. Blue eyes. 5'4". b. Ireland. Brass finisher. Co. D, 2nd US Vols. April 1865 escorting substitutes and drafted men to St. Louis. May-June 1865 absent sick. No diagnosis in CMSR. July 1865 discharged for disability.

France, Elijah. 64th Va. Mtd. Inf. Captured at Cumberland Gap. POW at Camp Douglas. Age 21. Black eyes. 5'6".

Illiterate. Co. K, 6th US Vols. July-August 1865 duty at Alkali (Fort Cottonwood) N.T. Deserted September 1865 at Alkali, owing $36 for equipment. Never caught.

Frazier, Daniel. 64th Va. Mtd. Inf. Captured at Cumberland Gap. POW at Camp Douglas. Age 22. Illiterate. Co. K, 6th US Vols. September-December 1865 duty at Morrow's Ranch, N.T. January 1866 QM duty at Fort Cottonwood. February-July 1866 Teamster. August-September 1866 company cook. Mustered out at Fort Kearney October 1866.

Frazier (Frasier, Frasher), George M. Residence Scott County, Va. Enlisted October 1861 in 21st Bn. Va. Infantry. Deserted November 1862. Transferred to Co. C, 64th Va. Mtd. Inf. Captured at Cumberland Gap. POW at Camp Douglas. 5th US Vols. Cannot locate CMSR. Mustered out as Sergeant. (George NMI Frazier, alias Isaac Rider, "unassigned US Vols." had a mother pension app dated 1906.)

Fry, John T. Co. D, 23rd Bn. Va. Inf. Enlisted May 1862 at Marion, Va. POW at Point Lookout. Age 18. Black eyes. 5'3". Illiterate. Co. E, 4th US Vols. At Fort Randall promoted to corporal December 1865. Mustered out at Fort Leavenworth June 1866. Invalid pension app 1885. d. January 11, 1915 Chilhowie, Va. Widow app 1915. Buried Riverside Cemetery, Smyth County. Wife Rebecca A. Gollehan (1847-1923).

Fry, Thomas M. 26th (Edgar's) Bn. Va. Inf. Captured at Winchester September 1864. POW at Rock Island. Age 22.

Blue eyes. 5'7". Co. C, 3rd US Vols. August 1865 cutting hay. Mustered out at Fort Leavenworth November 1865 owing for damaging the property of John Mattis. Invalid pension app 1901. Widow app undated.

Furry (Fury), Andrew J. Co. A, 8th Va. Inf. Captured at Gettysburg July 1863. POW at Fort Delaware, De. and Point Lookout. Age 19. Gray eyes. 5'5". Not vaccinated. Co. E, 1st US Vols. At Fort Rice until April 1865. May-July 1865 at Fort Benton, M.T. Mustered out as private at Fort Leavenworth November 1865. Invalid pension app 1898. d. December 1925 at Punxsutawney, Pa. Widow pension app 1926.

Gallyean, Samuel. 63rd (McMahon's) Va. Inf. 19-year old farmer, born Grayson, Va.. Blue eyes. 5'10". Co. D, 3rd US Vols. Absent sick August 1865 at Post Cottonwood, N.T. Mustered out November 1863 at Fort Leavenworth. Invalid pension app 1881. d. April 1921 at Loma, Co. Widow app 1921.

Galyer (Galyean, Galyon, Galyen), Jeremiah. Co. C, 63rd (McMahon's) Va. Inf. Captured at Resaca, Ga. POW at Alton, Il. Age 23. Blue eyes. 5'9". Illiterate. Musician. Co. C, 5th US Vols. December 1865-July 1866 company cook. Mustered out at Fort Kearney October 1866. 1881 invalid, widow, and minor pension apps.

Gentry, James M. Co. D, 23rd Va. Inf. Enlisted at Richmond May 1861. AWOL July 1861. AWOL November 1861. Deserted July 1862. In Castle Thunder Prison April 1863. Captured at Payne's Farm, Va. November 1863.

POW at Point Lookout. Age 30. Hazel eyes. 5'9". Co. C, 4th US Vols. Age 30. November 1864 company clerk. January 1865 d. of pneumonia, regimental hospital Norfolk, Va.

Gillispie (Gillespie), John. 50th Va. Inf. POW at Columbus, Oh. Age 36. Gray eyes. 5'7". Co. A, 6th US Vols. May-June 1865 teamster. August 1865 teamster at Powder River. September 1865 wagonmaster. November 1865 deserted at Camp Douglas, U.T., owing for Springfield rifle and canteen. Never caught. (There were two Camp Douglases.)

Goff, George W. Co. C, 42nd Va. Inf. Wounded at 2nd Manassas August 1862, at Antietam September 1862, and at Payne's Farm Va. Captured at Spotsylvania CH May 1864. POW at Point Lookout. POW at Elmira, N.Y. August 1864. Age 23. Blue eyes. 6'0". Had pneumonia 1861. Humerus fractured by ball. Vaccinated 3 times. Missing middle finger, left hand. Co. D, 1st US Vols. May 1865 detached service en route to Fort Sully, D.T. October 1865 detached service. Mustered out as private at Fort Leavenworth November 1865. (A George Washington Goff {clearly a different man} served in Parker's Va. Light Artillery, had excellent record, and was captured April 1865 at Harper's Farm, Va. He died in the Richmond Soldier's Home December 1899.)

Going(s), James E. Co, E. 11th Va. Inf. Captured May 1864 at Milford Station, Va. POW at Point Lookout. b. at Appomattox (!). Age 35. Blue eyes. 5'7". Illiterate. Co.

D, 4th US Vols. Deserted January 1865 at Norfolk, owing $55.55 for equipment.

Gregg, Omar (Owen) G. V. Co. K, 11th Va. Cav. Captured at Newtown, Va. while home AWOL October 1863. POW at Champ Chase. Then POW Rock Island January 1864. Age 18. Gray eyes. 5'10". Co. E, 2nd US Vols. May 1865 on escort to Fort Larned. June 1865 on escort to Indianola, Ks. Mustered out at Fort Leavenworth November 1865. Also served in 13th US Infantry 1865-1868. Invalid pension app 1908.

Grogg, Lewis G. Co. H, 63rd (McMahon's) Va. Inf. Had been Color Sergeant. Captured May 1864 Resaca, Ga. POW at Alton, Il. Age 23. Blue eyes. 5'9". Illiterate. Co. C, 5th US Vols. February-June 1866 in charge of artillery horses. Owed sutler S.N. Beall $5.00. Mustered in as Private and out as Corporal. October 1866 at Fort Kearney. Applied to replace a lost certificate 1886. Invalid pension app 1892. Widow app 1905.

Grubbs, Madison (Martin) L. 2nd Va. Inf. Enlisted Clarke Co. Va. Captured at Winchester, Va. POW at Camp Chase and Rock Island. Age 27. Blue eyes. 5'11". Illiterate. Co. G, 3rd US Vols. July 1865 escorting wagon train. Mustered out at Fort Leavenworth November 1865, owing $2.90 for damaging property of John Mattis.

Haley, Timothy. Co. B, 21st (Peter's) Va. Cav. Captured as Fisher's Hill, Va. September 1864. POW at Point Lookout. b. Ireland. Age 22. Blue eyes. 5'7". Illiterate. Co. B, 4th US Vols. June-November 1865 cook and baker. Mustered out as private June 1866 at Fort Leavenworth. Later served in Co. H, 7th US Cavalry and Co. K, 44th US Infantry. Invalid pension app 1884.

Hall, Robert E. Co. K, 42nd Va. Inf. He was born in Franklin, Va., February 22, 1843 and enlisted June 17, 1861 at Rocky Mount, Va. Occupation: farmer. He went AWOL September 26, 1861 and was still absent in February 1862. December 1863 court-martialed for AWOL. (No trial record in the General Orders of the Army of Northern Virginia.) He was never paid. Captured at Spotsylvania CH. POW at Point Lookout. Age 21. Blue eyes. 5'11". Vaccinated but "not taken." Co. D, 1st US Vols. No detached service noted in CMSR. Mustered out at Fort Leavenworth November 1865. Invalid pension app 1880. Hall moved to Union, Or. in 1892. He died May 16, 1931, of cancer of the stomach and uremia at Hot Lake, near Union, Or. His widow applied for a pension a few months after his death. His tombstone in Union Cemetery, Union, Or. is headed HALL, and records Mary A. [Loudermilk] 1847-1936 and Robert E. 1843-1931. He left eleven children, 42 grandchildren, 12 great-grandchildren, and one great-great-grandchild. His passing left the local GAR chapter with only one member. Union is a small farming town in eastern Oregon, whose lands are watered by Pyle's Creek.

Harris, Daw. Co. D, 64th Va. Mtd. Inf. Captured September 1863 Cumberland Gap. POW at Camp Douglas. Age 19.

CIVIL WAR VETERAN DIES

Union Now Has but One of Survivors of Struggle Left.

LA GRANDE, Or., May 16.—(AP)— Robert Edward Hall, 88, one of the two remaining veterans of the civil war living at Union, died today at Hot Lake. He was born in Virginia, and came west in 1892.

Mr. Hall is survived by his widow, 11 children, 42 grandchildren, 22 great-grandchildren and one great-great-grandchild.

Added by: Dena (Robertson) Knapp

Gray eyes. 5'10". Illiterate. Co. G, 5th US Vols. November-December 1865 at Beaver Creek Station. Promoted to corporal March 1866. Mustered out at Fort Kearney October 1866. Invalid pension app 1892. Widow app undated.

Harris, Peter L. 4th Va. Inf. 19-year old laborer. Enlisted April 1861. March 1862 captured and paroled at Kernstown, Va. Wounded and captured Gettysburg July 1863. POW Point Lookout. Age 21. Blue eyes. 6'0". Had been vaccinated. Had typhoid 1857. Co. B, 1st US Vols. Promoted to First Sergeant October 1864. Under arrest at Sioux City, Ia. Demoted to private. Mustered out at Fort Leavenworth November 1865.

Harwood, Joseph (James) E. Co. E, 63rd (McMahon's) Va. Inf. Captured at Chattahoochee River. POW at Camp Douglas. Age 33. Gray eyes. 5'7". Illiterate. Co. F, 5th US Vols. Deserted at Fort Riley April 1865, owing $4.90 to govt. and $2.50 to the sutler. Never caught. Died December 1920 Boone County, Tn.

Hawpe (Haupe), Adam (John) H. Co. A, 21st (Peter's) Va. Cav. Captured at Fisher's Hill, Va. September 1864. He has no CMSR for the 21st Cav. But they often fought near the Tennessee border and records from there are often missing. POW Point Lookout. Co. E, 4th US Vols. (There is an Adam H. Hawpe of Co. E, 5th Va. Infantry, who enlisted in April 1861, deserted, was hospitalized, furloughed and refused to re-enlist in April 1862. He deserted July 12, 1862 at Richmond.) These Hawpes are probably the same man. Invalid pension app 1890. Widow and child apps undated.

Haynes, Lafayette. Co. B, 51st Va. Inf. Captured at Missionary Ridge, Tn. November 1863. POW at Rock Island. Age 20. Dark eyes. 5'8". Illiterate. Co. C, 3rd US Vols. May 1865 at Fort Cottonwood, N.T. July 1865 sick. August 1865 cutting hay. November 1865 mustered out at Fort Leavenworth. Widow app 1890.

Heater, Jacob. Co. D, 31st Va. Inf. Enlisted at Gilmer, Va. Age 18. Captured July 1861 at Red House, Va. Exchanged August 1861. October 1862, hospital cook at Staunton, Va. Captured at Harris Farm, Va. May 1864. POW at Point Lookout. Age 20. Gray eyes. 6'0". Illiterate. Had been vaccinated. Co. I, 1st US Vols. June-July 1864 company cook. August 1864 sick in hospital, Camp Reno, Milwaukee. September 1864 deserted at Bloomington Ferry, Mn. Died May 11, 1930 at Confederate Soldiers Home, Richmond. There he sold cards with photos of himself. No record of a Federal pension.

Henderson, George. Co. B, 49th Va. Inf. POW at Point Lookout. Age 16. Blue eyes. 5'3". Illiterate. Had "dropsy" before the war. Never vaccinated. "I am in the habit of drinking." Co. I, 1st US Vols. Enlisted May 24, 1864. Deserted August 1, 1864, taking his musket and all his gear. (Served nine weeks.) Never caught.

Henderson, William. Co. C, 63rd (McMahon's) Va. Inf. Captured at Missionary Ridge, Tn. November 1863. POW at Rock Island. Age 31. Blue eyes. 5'11". Illiterate. Co. I, 6th US Vols. March 1865 owed $3.00 to sutler plus 65 cents for a lost canteen. July-August 1865 company cook. September-December 1865 detached service at Deer Creek Station, D.T. "40 miles west." January-February sick in hospital at Fort Laramie. March-April 1866 back at Deer Creek. August 1866 promoted to corporal. Mustered out at Fort Kearney October 1866. Invalid pension app 1907. There was a William Henderson in Co. H, 2nd US Vols.

Henson, Paul J. 39th Va. Inf. Captured at Pike Co. POW at Rock Island. Age 27. Gray eyes. 5'5". Illiterate. Co A, 3rd US Vols. CMSR entries: "Died at the Indiana House between Fort Riley and Fort Leavenworth, Kansas, April 16, 1865. He was left sick at that Place on march of the Regt. to Fort Kearney, N.T. March 17, 1865 . . . left sick on road & ordered to return to Gen'l Hospital, Ft. Leavenworth Mar. 17/65 . . . Died of disease at Mount Tarance Kan. Apr. 16/65 . . . May, 1865, April 16/65, Indianola House, Kansas, Died of disease . . .

Cause of casualty Typhus Fever . . . Place of death Mt. Torrence, Kans." The Kansas Historical Society's "Dead Town List" shows two Indianolas, in Butler and Shawnee counties. He is not listed at the Fort Worth National Cemetery. Widow app 1871.

Hicks (Hix), John C. 28th Va. Inf. POW at Point Lookout. Age 25. Blue eyes. 5'8". Illiterate. Had been vaccinated, both arms. Co. B, 1st US Vols. August-October 1865 company cook. Mustered out at Fort Leavenworth November 1865.

Higgins, Linville. Co. C, 63rd (McMahon's) Va. Inf. AWOL September 1863. Smallpox nurse March 1864. Captured at Dalton, Ga. POW at Rock Island. Age 28. Gray eyes. 5'6". Illiterate. Co. I, 2nd US Vols. Mustered out Fort Leavenworth November 1865.

Hipes, W. Preston. Co. K (F), 60th Va. Inf. (Wise Legion). Also Co. A, 22nd Va. Inf. Deserted and imprisoned at Wheeling, W.V. November 1862. Captured and exchanged through Cairo, Il. December 1862. Captured at Winchester (others say Fisher's Hill). POW at Point Lookout. Age 19. Gray eyes. 5'7". Illiterate. Co. D, 4th US Vols. October 1865 owed 95 cents for lost equipment. On QM duty November 1865-May 1866. Mustered out at Fort Leavenworth June 1866. Invalid pension app 1897. Died 1914, Troutville, Va. (Two different men?).

Hoback, Henry. Co. C, 50th Va. Inf. Enlisted July 1861. Sick in hospital with chronic dysentery November 1861.

Captured at Gettysburg. POW at Point Lookout. Age 23. Dark eyes. 5'8". Had been vaccinated. Co. F, 1st US Vols. Died of dysentery in regimental hospital at Norfolk, Va. July 1864. Personal effects: "none."

Hodges, Robert M. Co. D, 23rd Bn. Va. Inf. Enlisted July 1861. POW at Point Lookout. Age 21. Gray eyes. 5'2". Illiterate. Co. E, 4th US Vols. January-February 1866 and April 1866 QM duty. Mustered out at Fort Leavenworth June 1866. Died in 1900.

Holland, Joseph D. Co. F, 55th Va. Inf. Deserted at Chancellorsville May 1863. Captured August 1863 at Gloucester Point, Va. POW at Point Lookout. Age 20. Black eyes. 5'7". Had been vaccinated. Co. F, 1st US Vols. Promoted to corporal February 1864. October-November 1865 sick at Fort Leavenworth. December 1865 duty at HQ District of Kansas. January-March 1866 detached service. Mustered out as Sergeant April 1866 at Fort Leavenworth.

Hope, Thomas G. Co. H, 22nd Bn. Va. Inf. POW at Point Lookout .Age 27. Blue eyes. 5'7". Not vaccinated. Co. G, 1st US Vols. October 1864 "absent on Northern Stockade Line." November-December 1864 and April 1865 taking care of horses. June 1865 company cook. July-August 1865 QM Dept. Mustered out May 1866 Fort Leavenworth. Invalid pension app 1890.

Hotellen (Hotelen), Henry. Co. G, 38th (Pittsylvania) Va. Inf. POW at Point Lookout. Age 28. Gray eyes. 5'8". In CSA service had typhoid fever and fractured tarsal bone in one foot. Co. K, 1st US Vols. d. March 1865 of chronic diarrhea at Fort Rice. Reburied Custer Battlefield National Cemetery, site 194.

Hounshell (Houndshell), Jediah (Judedih, Judiah). G. Co. B, 50th Va. Inf. Enlisted June 1861. Deserted and returned July 1861. Captured Spotsylvania CH May 1864. POW at Point Lookout. Co. I, 1st US Vols. Cannot locate CMSR.

Howard, Harrison. Co. E, 47th Va. Inf. Enlisted June 1861. Residence Caroline County. AWOL July 1862. Captured at Gettysburg July 1863. POW at Point Lookout. Age 23. Blue eyes. 5'10". Vaccinated left arm. Illiterate. Co. E, 1st US Vols. Mustered out at Fort Leavenworth November 1865.

Howard, Horace E. Co. H, 28th Va. Inf. Captured at "Toneytown" (Taneytown) Md. July 1863. POW at Point Lookout. Age 18. Gray eyes. 5'8". Had scarlatina earlier. Scar left knee from gunshot wound. Co. D, 1st US Vols. Deserted at Benton Barracks, Mo. In April 1865 while at Prince Street Prison in Alexandria, Va.,wrote a two-page narrative. Paraphrase: I was at St. Louis with my regiment waiting to go to Fort Rice. I had permission to go into the city. I got drunk and missed the boat. Then I was sick and was placed in Hickory Street Hospital. I left without permission, took a boat north, but got off sick at St. Joseph, Mo. and was arrested there in hospital. I was sent to Fort Leavenworth, then to Myrtle Street Prison in St. Louis and then to

Annapolis and then to this place. I was doing my best to get back to my regiment. "No discharge furnished."

Hyden, Granville. Co. B, 64th Va. Mtd. Inf. Enlisted September 1861, age 23. Captured at Cumberland Gap September 1863. POW at Camp Douglas. Age 25. Blue eyes. 5'8". Illiterate. Co. G, 5th US Vols. April 1865 owed $2.50 to sutler at Fort Riley. December 1865 company cook. January 1866 teamster duty at Camp Hardwell, C.T. May 1866 deserted at Denver City, C.T. while on QM duty, owing govt. $57.00. 1899 married Dorothula in Lee County, Va.

Hyden, John M. 64th Va. Mtd. Inf. Captured at Cumberland Gap. POW at Camp Douglas. Age 30. Blue eyes. 5'8". Illiterate. Co. G, 5th US Vols. April 1865 promoted to corporal and owed sutler $3.00. Invalid pension app 1890. d. Oklahoma 1917.

Ingram, Charles H. Co. H, 55th Va. Inf. Captured at the Wilderness. POW at Point Lookout. Age 21. Brown eyes. 5'5". Had been vaccinated. Had "intermittent fever" in CSA. Co. I, 1st US Vols. July 1864 promoted to corporal. August 1864 promoted to sergeant. June 1865 reduced to private. August 1865 promoted to corporal. September 1865 post orderly. May 1866 mustered out at Fort Leavenworth.

Jackson, Morris (Morris Jackson). 64th Va. Mtd. Inf. Captured at Rappahannock. POW at Point Lookout. Co. A, 1st US Vols. See under Morris, Jackson, Morris being the last name.

Jackson, Morris. POW at Camp Douglas. Age 19. Blue eyes. 5'6". Illiterate. Co. G, 5th US Vols. June 1865 owed $2.50 to sutler at Fort Riley. March 1866 deserted at Camp Wardwell, C.T. Owed $28.64 for gun and cartridge box. Arrested August 1866.

Jenkins, Isaac C. 10th Va. Inf. Captured at Bermuda N.S. POW at Point Lookout. Age 20. Blue eyes. 5'7". Illiterate. Co. E, 4th US Vols. Deserted February 1865 by escaping from confinement at Norfolk. Never caught. 1880 census shows six children. Wife Elizabeth. 1880 applied for Virginia Confederate pension.

Johnson, Martin C. 62nd Va. Mtd. Inf. Resident of Barbour County. Deserted September 17, 1863 in Braxton County. Captured at Braxton Co. POW at Rock Island. Age 22. Black eyes. 5'10". Co. F, 3rd US Vols. September 1865 sent to Fort Kearney for discharge on account of sickness. "Hemorrhage of the lungs." (Probably tuberculosis.)

Johnson, Minor. 11th Va. Inf. Absent sick September 1862. AWOL May-June 1863. Captured at Braxton Co. POW at New Berne, then Rock Island. Age 21. Co. A, 1st US Vols. Cannot locate CMSR. Alive in 1891.

Johnson, Peter W. 35th (White's) Va. Cav. Bn. Captured at Chester Gap. POW at Point Lookout. Age 18. Hazel eyes. 5'6". Co. D, 1st US Vols. May 1864 "permanent guard duty Portsmouth Ferry, Norfolk." Under arrest in guard house August 1864 through February 1865. March 1865 convicted of AWOL at St. Louis and sentenced to two months hard labor. (NARA RG153 File folder MM1698.) October 1865 detached service. Mustered out November 1865.

Jones, George G. 64th Va. Mtd. Inf. POW at Camp Douglas. Age 39. Blue eyes. 5'4". Illiterate. Co. G, 5th US Vols. Enlisted April 1865. Deserted June 1865 at Cottonwood Crossing, Ks. , taking his musket. He owed the Fort Riley sutler $2.50.

Jones, Stephen (Stephan). 55th Va. Inf. Captured at Mine Run. POW at Point Lookout. Age 23. Blue eyes. 5'8". Illiterate. Co. G, 1st US Vols. August 1864-January 1865 on detached duty as a pioneer at regimental HQ, Fort Riley, while the rest of his company was at Milwaukee. June 1865- April 1866 sick in hospital at St. Louis. While he was in hospital his company was at Fort Fletcher. He owed the hospital sutler $35.00 (roughly $800 in today's money). Discharged August 1866. No diagnosis in CMSR.

Judson, William. Co. B, 5th Va. Inf. Captured at Frederick City. POW at Point Lookout. Age 20, Blue eyes. 6'0". While in CSA service had "brain fever." Never vaccinated. Co. A, 1st US Vols. Deserted at Milwaukee August 1864, taking knapsack, haversack, and eagle. Possibly in prison in Norfolk later in August.

Keith (Kieth, Key, Keath), Anderson G. 26th (Edgar's) Bn. Va. Inf. Soldiers of this name served from North Carolina and South Carolina. POW at Point Lookout. Age 19. Blue eyes. 5'9". Illiterate. Co. D, 4th US Vols. October-

December sick in hospital at Portsmouth, Va. January 1865-May 1866 no record of detached service. Mustered out at Fort Leavenworth June 1866. Invalid pension app 1889. Widow Mary app 1910.

Kemp, John W. 45th Va. Inf. Captured September 1864 at Winchester. POW at Point Lookout. Age 23. Blue eyes. 6'2". Illiterate. Co. C, 4th US Vols. February 1865 company cook. July-August 1865 carpenter at Fort Rice. Mustered out at Fort Leavenworth July 1866. 1905 invalid pension app. 1922 widow app.

Kirk, Benjamin. Co. G, 48th Va. Inf. Enlisted July 1861 Lee County, Va. Hospitalized 5 months in 1863. Captured May 1864 at Spotsylvania CH. POW at Point Lookout. Age 27. Black eyes. 5'11". Smallpox 1863. Co. K, 1st US Vols. May 1865 sick at Fort Rice. Sent to St. Louis. June 16, 1865 died of chronic diarrhea on steamer *Yellowstone* en route to US General Hospital at St. Louis. "Good character."

Kropff (Cropp), Harvey D. 54th Va. Inf. Age 18. Dark eyes. 5'7". Illiterate. POW at Camp Douglas. Co. I, 6th US Vols. March 1865 detached service at Horse Shoe, D.T. August 1865 to July 1866 Fort Laramie, D.T. Mustered out at Fort Kearney October 1866. 1882 invalid pension app.

Lake, Charles. Co. C, 18th Bn. Va. Hvy. Arty. Court-martialed February 1864. POW at Point Lookout. Age 35. Blue eyes. 5'6". Has had the "horrors" (delirium tremens). Has had smallpox. Illiterate. Co. G, 1st US Vols.

Deserted August 1864 at Milwaukee, taking his Enfield rifle. Never caught.

Lambert, Jackson. 63rd (McMahon's) Va. Inf. POW at Alton, Il. Age 30. Blue eyes. 5'8". Co. C, 5th US Vols. No record of detached service. Mustered out at Fort Kearney October 1866. 1892 invalid pension app, living in Tn.

Lambert, John W. Co. F, 22nd Va. Cav. (Bowen's Regt.) POW at Point Lookout. Age 20. Blue eyes. 5'7". Co. D, 4th US Vols. June 1865 sick at Fort Sully. September 1865 transferred to General Hospital Sioux City where he died of typhoid fever in October 1865. His mother applied for a Union pension in 1892. Wife Mary applied for a Virginia pension in 1917.

Lancey (Laney), Robert K. 64th Va. Mtd. Inf. Enlisted April 1862. Deserted and returned June 1863. Captured at Cumberland Gap September 1863. POW at Camp Douglas. Age 34. Brown eyes. 5'11". Co. H, 5th US Vols. Deserted June 14, 1865 at Chapman Creek, Ks., taking Springfield rifle and tent.

Land, Napoleon B. Co. F, 6th Va. Inf. Captured and exchanged September 1862 at Crampton's Gap, Md. Captured July 1863 at Falling Waters, Va. POW at Point Lookout. Age 21. Hazel eyes. 5'7". Had been vaccinated. Co. L, 1st US Vols. September-October 1864 "absent on Northern Stockade Line." In October 1865 "in confinement." In January 1866 in confinement again, charged with violation of Article Seven. "By conduct and words show mutinous actions tending to entice others, <u>to wit</u>: throwing his musket into the snow and kicking it saying I'll be damned if I carry this damned thing any more or words to that effect. This at or near Big Creek Station, Smoky Hill Route, Kansas, on or about the night of the 26th of December 1865." (This trial is not in NARA RG153.) In April 1866 he was on detached service. He was mustered out in May 1866 at Fort Leavenworth. In 1870 he was living at Fort Ripley, Mn.

Lane, Gordon H. Co. C, 54th Va. Inf. Enlisted September 1861. Captured at Atlanta, Ga. POW at Camp Douglas, Il. Age 20. Brown eyes. 5'9". Illiterate. Co. K, 6th US Vols. July 1865 escort duty to Julesburg. August-September at Bishop's Ranch, N.T. October 1865 company cook. November-December 1865 at Baker's Ranch, N.T. February-March 1866 "cutting timber in cañons." April-September 1866 escort for surveying party. Mustered out at Fort Kearney October 1866. Invalid pension app 1892. Widow app 1917. A Gordon Lane (No H.) applied for a Virginia pension in 1910.

Lane, Martin. Co. D, 64th Va. Mtd. Inf. Enlisted August 1862 at Saltville, Va. Captured September 1863 Cumberland Gap. POW at Camp Douglas. Age 30. Gray eyes. 5'7". Co. G, 5th US Vols. September 1864 company cook. October-December 1864 butcher. July-August 1866 detached service at Fort McPherson, N.T. Mustered out at Fort Kearney October 1866. Invalid pension app 1888.

Lane, Nathan B. Co. C, 64th Va. Mtd. Inf. Enlisted April 1862 in 21st Bn. Va. Inf. Discharged for disability September 1862. February 1863 enlisted in 64th Va. Mtd. Inf. Captured Cumberland Gap September 1863. POW Camp Douglas. Age 28. Blue eyes. 5'8". Co. G, 5th US Vols. June 1865 owed $3.00 to sutler at Fort Riley. November-December 1865 detached service at Beaver Creek Station, C.T. July-August 1866 detached service at Fort McPherson, N.T. Mustered out at Fort Kearney October 1866. (Brother of Martin Lane?). Invalid pension app 1890.

Lawson, Henry P. 64th Va. Mtd. Inf. Same particulars as Nathan Lane. POW at Camp Douglas. Age 23. Hazel eyes. 5'5". Co. K, 6th US Vols. July 1865 detailed to Alkali Station. October-November 1865 company cook. January-May 1866 in charge of company kitchen. June 1866 at Fort McPherson his wife was appointed company laundress. July-August 1866 in charge of "govt. wood." Mustered out at Fort Kearney October 1866.

Leady (Leedy), Pierson (Pearson) C. Co. F, 45th Va. Inf. Enlisted May 1861. Sick August 1861. Captured September 1864 at Winchester. POW at Point Lookout. Age 22. Blue eyes. 5' 10". Illiterate. Co. C, 4th US Vols. February 1865 promoted to corporal. May 1865 deserted and caught at Sioux City. Sentenced to two years hard labor at Fort Sully. Discharged at Fort Leavenworth June 1866.

Ligget (Leggett), John R. 36th Bn. Va. Cav. (? 14th Va. Cav.) POW at Point Lookout. Age 26. Gray eyes. 5'5". Had pneumonia 1864. Had been vaccinated. Had piles. Co. E, 1st US Vols. May 1865 permanent guard duty at Portsmouth Ferry Boat Landing, Norfolk. May 1865 carrying dispatches from Fort Rice to Fort Sully. June 1865 back at Fort Rice. August 1865 owes 95 cents for lost haversack, and on duty as herder. Mustered out at Fort Leavenworth November 1865.

Loverne, George. 63rd (McMahon's) Va. Inf. POW at Rock Island. Age 26. Hazel eyes. 5'10". Illiterate. Co. F, 3rd US Vols. May-September 1865 with QM Dept. working on adobe buildings. Mustered out at Fort Leavenworth November 1865, owing $2.90 for damaging the property of John Mattis.

Loverne, Stith. 63rd (McMahon's) Va. Inf. POW at Rock Island. Age 37. Blue eyes. 5'10". Illiterate. Co. F, 3rd US Vols. August 1865 promoted to corporal. May-July 1865 working on adobe buildings. Mustered out at Fort Leavenworth November 1865 owing money for damaging property of John Mattis.

Mahoney, James. 52nd Va. Inf. POW at Point Lookout. Age 22. Blue eyes. Illiterate. b. in Ireland. Enlisted in 2nd US Vols which became the 4th US Vols, Co. B. August-September 1865 company baker. November 1865 to (illegible). 1866 QM duty. April 1866 promoted to corporal. Mustered out at Fort Leavenworth June 1866.

Later joined the 7th US Cavalry. Invalid pension app 1906. Widow app 1916.

Marks, Joseph. Co. D, 44th Va. Inf. Captured Spotsylvania CH May 1864. POW Point Lookout. Age 17. Blue eyes. 5'7". Illiterate. Had been vaccinated. Had diarrhea in CSA service. Co. I, 1st US Vols. April-May 1865 QM duty. June 1865 sick. Discharged sick July 1865 at Fort Snelling, Mn. Invalid pension app 1903. (Alias John Foster.)

Marshall, James R. Co. I, 63rd (McMahon's) Va. Inf. Enlisted April 1862. Smallpox July 1863. Deserted February 1864. POW at Rock Island. Age 23. Dark eyes. 5'11". Illiterate. Co. G, 2nd US Vols. September 1865 escort to Indian Commission. Mustered out at Fort Leavenworth November 1865. Invalid pension app in 1925 and died in 1932. (Other men by the same name seem to have died in Virginia in 1918 and in Missouri in 1920, and seem to have served in the Jackson Light Artillery and the 50th Va. Infantry.)

Martin, Henry. Co. E, 47th Va. Inf. Enlisted March 1862, Caroline County. May 1863 court-martialed for AWOL. Five days later, captured at Port Royal, Va. POW at Point Lookout. Age 26. Hazel eyes. 5'6". He had intermittent fever in CSA service. Had been vaccinated. June 1864 mustered into Co. H, 1st US Vols. (There is also a Henry Martin in Co. I, 1st US Vols.) June 1864 sick in hospital at Norfolk. August 1864 to April 1865 and June to October 1865 hospitalized at St. Louis for chronic diarrhea. Regiment mustered out

November 1865 but he was discharged from the hospital in January 1866. Invalid pension app 1891. d. 1903 at Affton, Mo. Widow Harriet app 1904. Buried August 14, 1903, for \$3, in Potter's Field, Union Cemetery, Kansas City, Mo. No trace of gravestone.

Martin, Robert. Co. C, 57th Va. Inf. Enlisted June 1861. Deserted and returned August 1863. Deserted May 1864. Captured September 1864 at Strasburg Va. POW at Point Lookout. Age 23. Blue eyes. 5'8". Illiterate. 2nd US Vols became the 4th US Vols. Martin in Co. D. Absent sick September-October 1865 at Sioux City. Discharged there November 1865. Invalid pension app 1884. d. 1910 Nowlin's Mill, Va. Widow app 1910.

Matheny, John H. Co. H, 25th (Heck's) Va. Inf. Covington Va. POW at Point Lookout. Age 22. Gray eyes. 5'10". Had been vaccinated. Co. H, 1st US Vols. September 1864 promoted to corporal. Mustered out at Fort Leavenworth November 1865. Invalid pension app 1891. d. at Rockbridge Baths, Va. 1920. Widow app 1920.

McCrackin (McCracken), James K. 26th (Edgar's) Bn. Va. Inf. Co. POW at Point Lookout. Age 35. Hazel eyes. 5'6". Illiterate. Co. B, 4th US Vols. May 1865 deserted at Elmira, N.Y. Never caught.

McDaniel(s), Charles H. (or F.) Co. D, 63rd (McMahon's) and 24th Va. Inf. Captured May 1864 Cassville, Ga. POW at Rock Island. Age 18. Gray eyes. 5'11". Co. H, 3rd US Vols. May-August detached service at Valley Station (state not given). Mustered out at Fort Leavenworth August

1865. Charged $2.90 for damaging property of John Mattis.

McKenzie (McKinney, McKinzie, McKinzey), David. Co. D, 64th Va. Mtd. (Had been transferred from 21st Bn. Va. Inf.) Captured at Cumberland Gap September 1863. POW Camp Douglas. Age 29. Black eyes. 5'8". Enlisted April 1865 in Co. G, 5th US Vols. Promoted to corporal April 1865. August 1865 owed $3.00 to sutler at Fort Riley. Mustered out at Fort Kearney, N.T. October 1866. Invalid pension app 1890. Widow (Mary) app 1897.

McPeak, James. Co. C, 36th Va. Cav. Sgt. POW at Rock Island. Age 36. Blue eyes. 5'11". Co. A, 3rd US Vols. Appointed corporal February 1865. Deserted August 1865 at Elm Creek Station, N.T., taking with him two Enfield rifles. Charges dropped 1885. In 1916 he wants a copy of his discharge. No pension app.

Meadows, Harvey D. Co. E, 17th Va. Cav. POW at Point Lookout. Age 27. Blue eyes. 5'6". Had been vaccinated. Illiterate. Co. B, 1st US Vols. August 1865 on detached service at Fort Union, M.T. Mustered out at Fort Leavenworth November 1865. Invalid pension app 1890.

Meeks, Newell J. Co. D, 44th Va. Inf. Captured May 1864 at Spotsylvania CH. POW at Point Lookout. Age 17. Gray eyes. 5'7". Had rheumatism in CSA service. Vaccination "never took." A week after capture joined Co. I, 1st US Vols. Three months later deserted from US

Vols. at Pasquotank, N.C., taking his musket and accoutrements. d. 1921?

Miller, David. Co. E, 64th Va. Mtd. Inf. Resident of Scott County, Va. Enlisted April 1862 at Moccasin Gap, Va. In 21st Bn. Va. Inf. December 1862 transferred to 64th Va. Mtd. Inf. Court-martialed November 1862 (forfeit one month pay). Captured at Cumberland Gap. POW at Camp Douglas. Age 21. Blue eyes. 5'5". Illiterate. Co. G, 5th US Vols. August 1865 owed sutler $2.50 at Fort Riley. August 1866 detached service at Fort McPherson, N.T. Mustered out October 1866 at Fort Kearney. Invalid pension app 1892.

Miller, George P. 64th Va. Mtd. Inf. POW at Camp Douglas. Age 27. Hazel eyes. 5'7". Illiterate. Co. K, 6th US Vols. August-September 1865 detached service at Elkhorn, N.T. October-December 1865 daily duty as herder. January 1866 at Post Cottonwood, N.T. March 1866 attending a court-martial at Fort Kearney. April-June 1866 company cook. August 1866 his parents wrote to the Secretary of War asking that George come home. Dad is 1812 war veteran. He and mom are both old and weak. Fifteen neighbors at Cumberland Gap attest the facts. George is mustered out with his regiment October 1866 at Fort Kearney. Invalid pension app 1887.

Miller, William H. 26th (Edgar's) Bn. Va. Inf. POW at Point Lookout. Age 18. Gray eyes. 5'11". Co. E, 4th US Vols. October-November 1865 and March-May 1866 QM duty. Mustered out at Fort Leavenworth June 1866.

Minnic(k), Isaac. Co. B, 63rd (McMahon's) Va. Inf. Enlisted June 1863 at Bristol, Tn. Captured Missionary Ridge November 1863. POW Rock Island. Age 19. Light eyes. 5'4". Illiterate. Co. I, 2nd US Vols. Mustered out at Fort Leavenworth November 1865. Invalid pension app 1890.

Mitchem (Mitcham, Micham), Jacob S. Co. C, 37th Va. Inf. Co. G, 1st US Vols. Cannot locate CMSR.

Money (Monney), Perry (Terry). 64th Va. Mtd. Inf. POW at Camp Douglas. Age 32. Gray eyes. 5'8". Illiterate. Co. F, 5th US Vols. AWOL August 1865 at Fort Riley, owing sutler $2.50. September 1865 deserted on the march near Fort Kearney, taking a tent. Never caught.

Moore, Andrew. 31st Va. Cav. b. Pike, Ky. POW at Rock Island. Age 21. Hazel eyes. 5'8". Illiterate. Co. A, 3rd US Vols. May-June 1865 on detached service "guarding M station O.M.L.R." Owes sutler $10. Mustered out at Fort Leavenworth November 1865.

Moore, William. In the CMSRs of Virginia Confederates there are 140 men named William Moore. Higher numbered units such as the 31st Va. Cavalry (which morphed into the 40th Va. Cavalry) have often irregular records. Further, it's not clear why some of these men appear in a list of galvanized Virginians. *Caveat lector.*

Moore, William. 31st Va. Cav. b. Washington, Tn. POW at Point Lookout. Age 21. Light eyes. 5'6" Illiterate. Had been vaccinated. Co. B, 1st US Vols. June-July Officer's waiter (!). May 1865 gardener. August 1865 detached service at Fort Union, M.T. October 1865 detached service at Fort Rice. Mustered out at Fort Leavenworth November 1865. Writes to pension bureau 1892.

Moore, William. (Confederate unit unknown) POW at Rock Island. Age 19. Dark eyes. 5'6". Illiterate. Born in Pike, Ky. Co. A, 3rd US Vols. May-June 1865 "guarding M station O.L.M.R." Mustered out November 1865 at Fort Leavenworth, owing money for the destruction of the property of John Mattis.

Moore, William C. b. Hickman, Tn. POW at Rock Island. Age 20. Gray eyes. 5'9". <u>Not</u> illiterate. Co. A, 3rd US Vols. May 1865 "guarding M station on O.L.M.R." Mustered out at Fort Leavenworth November 1865, owing money for the destruction of property of John Mattis.

Moore, William D. b. Green County, Tn. POW at Camp Douglas. Age 20. Blue eyes. 5'10". Illiterate. Co. B, 6th US Vols. Enlisted April 1865. May 1865 sick at Camp Fry. July 1865 at Beaver Creek Station, C.T. September 1865 deserted at Camp Wardwell, C.T., taking his musket and all equipment. Never caught.

Moore, William H. b. Peckingham, N.C. POW at Rock Island. Age 19. Hazel eyes. 5'4". Illiterate. Co. H, 2nd US Vols. June-July 1865 escort to Fort Lyon. July 1865 on duty as a herder, drowned in Pawnee Fork near Fort Larned.

Moore, William R. b. Hopkins County, Ky. POW at Camp Morton. Age 19. Blue eyes. 5'9". Illiterate. Co, G. 6th US Vols. September 1865-February 1866 on guard at

Laramie Peak Sawmill, D.T. March-April 1866 escort for train at Fort Reno. May 1866 on daily duty with Lieut. [Stephen] Porter. Mustered out at Fort Kearney October 1866. (Prisoner of War memorandum notes that he was captured at Jackson, Miss. July 17, 1863, and confined at Camp Morton a month later. Enlisted USA March 24, 1865. "Pens. 414069 (152421) Conf. Arch. Mar. 19/90. Co. E, 8 Ky. Inf." The digitized Confederate records have only a single card: "Moore, William R. Co. F, 8th Kentucky Mounted Infantry. Cards filed with, Moore, W. R.")

Morgan, William B. Co. K, 50th Va. Inf. Enlisted June 1861 at Wise CH. Captured at Culp's Hill, Gettysburg July 3, 1863. Age 37. Blue eyes. 5'11". Had typhoid 1863. POW at Point Lookout. Co. C, 1st US Vols. Died of secondary syphilis at Fort Rice, March 1865, owing sutler $15. No syphilis noted in US enlistment exam. (See author's book, *Civil War Venereal Disease Hospitals*.)

Morris, Jackson. 64th Va. Mtd. Inf. POW at Point Lookout. Age 22. Hazel eyes. 5'4". Had Yellow Fever 1861. Had been vaccinated. Co. A, 1st US Vols. October 1864 deserted at Fort Ridgeley, Mn. taking his Enfield rifle and all gear. October 1865 captured at Fort Snelling. November 1865 in arrest at Fort Fletcher. Hand-written trial transcript in CMSR. Dishonorably discharged.

Moses, James W. 6th Va. Cav. Captured at Weldon Railroad. POW at Point Lookout. Age 32. Blue eyes. 5'10".

Illiterate. Co. C, 4th US Vols. Deserted December 1864 at Norfolk. Never caught. (The only Moses in Michael P. Musick's *Sixth Virginia Cavalry* is W. A. Moses, who was in Co. F, and was paroled 5/16/65.)

Mullins, Hezekiah. 59th Va. Inf. POW at Point Lookout. Age 30. Brown eyes. 5'10". Had been vaccinated. Had "fever" in CSA. b. Hancock, Tenn. Illiterate. Co. I, 1st US Vols. July 1864 provost duty. January-February 1865 company cook. April-May 1865 QM duty. June 1865 in hospital Fort Snelling. No diagnosis in CMSR. Discharged July 1865.

Munsy (Muncy), James F. 54th Va. Inf. POW at Camp Douglas. Age 19. Blue eyes. 5'6" (6'0"). Co. I, 5th US Vols. May-June 1865 "coms'y Sergt." Deserted October 1865 at Fort Riley. Never caught.

Muntzing (Munsong), Henry (Heinrich). Co. F, 18th Va. Cav. Previously Imboden Rangers. Captured and exchanged November 1862. Age 17. Hazel eyes. Captured again August 1863 at his home, Frederick County, Va. POW at Rock Island. "I'm tired of the Confederacy. I just want to go home." Sick with parotitis (mumps?) at Rock Island. Co. K, 2nd US Vols. April 1865 on duty with battery. May 1865 with battery at Fort Zarah (or Larned). (Came on ship from Bremen 1856.) Mustered out at Fort Leavenworth November 1865. Invalid pension app 1895.

Murphy, Francis B. 62nd Va. Mtd. Inf. POW at Rock Island. Age 26. Hazel eyes. 5'7". Co. B, 2nd US Vols. No detached service in CMSR. Mustered out at Fort Leavenworth November 1865.

Murray, John. Co. F, 41st Va. Cav. (41st Battalion Va. Cavalry, White's Battalion.) Rank: corporal. Age 24. Gray eyes. 6'0". October 1863 in prison at Wheeling, Va. Sent to Camp Chase November 1863. Transferred to Rock Island January 1864. There were John Murrays in the 2nd, 3rd, and 4th US Vols. None of these match the age or height noted in the 41st Va. Cav.

Neikirk (Nikerck, Niekirk), James P. 23rd Bn. Va. Inf. POW at Point Lookout. Age 18. Blue eyes. 5'4" (also noted as 5'8") b. Smith, Va. Illiterate. Co. A, 4th US Vols. Deserted May 1865 from steamer *Mars* on the Missouri River en route from St. Louis to Iowa. 1888 given honorable discharge.

Nelson, Isom. 63rd (McMahon's) Va. Inf. POW at Camp Douglas. Age 31. Hazel eyes. 5'10". Co. I, 6th US Vols. June 1865 lost canteen and owed sutler $3.00. September 1865 detached service at Deer Creek Station, D.T. "40 miles west." April-June 1866 at Fort Casper D.T. July 1866 duty at Bridges Ferry, D.T. Mustered out at Fort Kearney October 1866. Invalid pension app 1888.

Nelson, John R. Co. F, 28th Va. Inf. He appears in the Denney roster but was at Appomattox at the surrender.

Nelson, John S. (CSA unit not clear.) POW at Rock Island. Age 23, Blue eyes. 5'5". b. Washington, Tn. Illiterate. Co. K, 2nd US Vols. April 1865 post teamster. May-June 1865

QM work at Fort Zarah. September 1865 assigned to Ordnance Dept. Mustered out at Fort Leavenworth November 1865.

Nelson, Thomas A. Co. K, 54th Va. Inf. Captured July 3, 1864 at Marietta, Ga. POW at Camp Douglas. Age 23. Gray eyes. 5'9". Co. I, 6th US Vols. Sick in hospital Fort Laramie August 1865 to June 1866. July 1866 on duty at Bridge's Ferry, D.T. September 1865 and January-February 1866 sick in hospital at Cottonwood Springs. February 1866 sick in hospital at Fort Leavenworth. March-April 1866 sick in hospital at Fort McPherson. May-June 1866 sick in hospital at Fort Leavenworth. Mustered out at Fort Kearney October 1866. No diagnosis in CMSR.

Neville (Nevill), Lewis (Louis) C. (V). Co. D, 11th Va. Inf. POW at Point Lookout. Age 20. Blue eyes. 5'10". Co. D, 2nd US Vols (later 4th USV). Appointed 2nd Sergeant. No detached service in CMSR. Mustered out at Fort Leavenworth June 1866.

Newlin, Joseph. Co. I, 6th Va. Inf. Captured at Salinaville, Oh. POW at Champ Chase, escaped. Caught, sent to Rock Island. Age 35. Dark eyes. 5'8". Co. D, 3rd US Vols. April 1865 company cook. May-June 1865 on duty at Gillman's Station, N.T. September 1865 sick at Post Cottonwood. Mustered out at Fort Leavenworth November 1865.

Niswander (Nisnander), John W. Drafted into Co. H, 10th Va. Inf. POW at Point Lookout. Age 18. Hazel eyes. 5'6".

Illiterate. Had been vaccinated. Blacksmith. Co. H, 1st US Vols. July 1864 guard at Portsmouth Ferry. June 1865 at Fort Rice, sent to hospital at St. Louis. Discharged June 1865 because of cataract, right eye. (Doctor at Point Lookout stated "eyes normal.") Owed sutler $2.00. m. Lydia. Widow pension app 1925.

Odell, Theophilus. Co. C, 48th Va. Inf. b. Taswell, Va. Enrolled at Scott County. Captured at Waterloo, Pa. July 4, 1863. POW at Point Lookout. Age 24. Brown eyes. 5'9". Had been vaccinated. Illiterate. Co. B, 1st US Vols. No detached service in CMSR. Mustered out at Fort Leavenworth November 1865. d. 1900.

Osborne (Osburn), Thomas. Co. E, 16th Va. Cav. POW at Point Lookout. Age 23. Blue eyes. 5'8". Had typhoid 1863. Had been vaccinated. Co. G, 1st US Vols. September-October 1864 absent on Northern Stockade Line. January-April 1865 taking care of horses. May-October 1865 company cook. November-December 1865 officer's cook. February-March 1866 officer's cook at Fort Fletcher. Mustered out May 1866 at Fort Leavenworth.

Oslin, James M. 44th Va. Inf. Wounded at Fredericksburg 1862. POW at Point Lookout. Age 27. Gray eyes. 5'8". Miller. Had typhoid 1862. Two broken ribs 1854. Had been vaccinated. Co. E, 1st US Vols. September 1865 deserted at Fort Rice, taking his musket. Never caught. 1889 charges dropped, discharge issued.

Oslin (Oslen, Osslin), Samuel S. (L., S.S., S.J.). Co. B, 41st Va. April 1862 absent sick. August 1862 in Chimborazo Hospital one week for acute diarrhea. September 1862 in Winder Hospital four days. January 1863 in hospital with bronchitis at Charlottesville, Va.. January-May 1863 in hospital at Scottsville, Va. July 1863 AWOL. Captured at Gettysburg July 4, 1863. POW at Point Lookout. Age 19. Hazel eyes. 5'10". "Had typhoid 1862." Illiterate. Co. E, 1st US Vols. In hospital at St. Louis August 1864-April 1865. May-June 1865 on duty at "C.S. Depot." September 1865 sent "down river" from Fort Rice to hospital at Sioux City (and/or St. Louis). Received "convalescent discharge." (Examiner at Point Lookout had pronounced him fit for duty.) Invalid pension app 1888. Widow pension app 1908.

Palmer, Samuel P. (R.). Co. A, 54th Va. Inf. Enlisted at Jacksonville with $50 bounty. Captured near Atlanta July 20, 1864. POW at Camp Douglas. Age 25. Blue eyes. 5'6". Co. H, 5th US Vols. July 1865 escorting wagon train to Fort Lyon. August 1865 owed $2.50 to sutler at Fort Riley. Deserted November 4, 1865 at Elm Creek, taking his Springfield musket and all his gear. Never caught.

Patrick, Greenberry (Granbery). 45th Va. Inf. POW at Point Lookout. Age 20. Blue eyes. 6'1". Illiterate. Co. D, 4th US Vols. November 1865 at Fort Randall. December 1865-May 1866 company cook. Mustered out June 1866 at Fort Leavenworth. (A conflicting record says discharged for disability November 8, 1865, at Sioux City.) 1913 in National Home for Disabled Volunteer Veterans, Tennessee.

Patterson, William J. Co. H, 21st Va. Inf. Enlisted at Pittsylvania. February 1862 sick at Winchester. AWOL June 1863. "Due thirty dollars for being arrested whilst absent without leave." November 1863 captured at Mine Run. December 1863 reported AWOL again. Charged for lost Enfield musket. POW at Point Lookout. Age 20. Dark eyes. 5'5". Had been vaccinated. Co. F, 1st US Vols. June-July 1864 QM duty. October 1864-April 1865 QM duty at Fort Rice. May 1865 drum corps at Fort Rice. October-September 1865 detached service at Fort Rice. December 1865-March 1866 post butcher at Fort Fletcher. Mustered out at Fort Leavenworth May 1866.

Patton (Patten), James R. Co. A, 63rd (McMahon's) Va. Inf. Enlisted March 1862. $50 bounty. Deserted July 1862. AWOL August 1863-January 1864. Captured at Calhoun, Ga. May 1864. POW at Rock Island. Co. K, 2nd US Vols. Cannot locate CMSR. He seems to have an invalid pension app in 1883, a widow's app in 1919, and a Confederate pension app in 1900.

Pendleton, William. E. Co. E, 7th Va. Inf. Conscript. Enrolled at Culpeper CH. Listed as AWOL May 19, 1864. Captured at North Anna May 22, 1864. POW at Point Lookout. Age 25. Gray eyes. 5'8". Had been vaccinated. Co. K, 1st US Vols. Confined three days at Fort Rice for stealing whiskey. August 1864 lost his canteen. Sick at Fort Rice May 1865. Mustered out at Fort Leavenworth November 1865.

Pettus (Peters, Pettis), John E. Co. E, 11th Va. Inf. September 1862 in hospital at Culpeper with "vulnus sclopeticum" (gunshot wound). September 1862 deserted. January 1863 returned. June 1863 "missing." July 3, 1863, captured at Gettysburg, in the middle of Pickett's Charge. POW at Point Lookout. Age 39. Blue eyes. 5'9". Tobacconist. Co. D, 4th US Vols. QM duty November 1864. Deserted at Norfolk December 1864. Never caught.

Petty, Mathew M. 30th Bn. Va. S. S. POW at Point Lookout. Age 23. Dark eyes. 5'8". Had been vaccinated. Had pneumonia 1863. Co. G, 1st US Vols. August 1864-September 1865 pioneer duty at Fort Rice. October 1865 AWOL. November 1865 deserted at Salt Creek, Ks. on the march from Fort Leavenworth to Fort Fletcher, taking his tent and canteen. 1885 charge of desertion dropped. Invalid pension app 1886. d. November 15, 1908. Buried Oakridge Baptist Cemetery, Lewis County, Ky. Widow app 1909.

Phipps, Elcanor (Alchano, Elkanah). Co. B, 64th Va. Mtd. Inf. AWOL December 1862. Present January 1863. Captured at Cumberland Gap September 9, 1863. POW at Camp Douglas. Age 20. Gray eyes. 5'9". Illiterate. Co. G, 5th US Vols. November 1865 escorting wagon train to Beaver Creek. February 1866 cutting wood on the

"Bayon." May 1866 QM duty. Mustered out at Fort Kearney October 1866.

Poteet (Palter), Jacob O. Co. K, 54th Va. Inf. b. Roanoke. Enlisted at Salem October 1861. Captured at Atlanta July 20, 1864. POW at Camp Douglas. Age 21. Black eyes. 5'4". Illiterate. Co. F, 5th US Vols. November 1865 nurse at Post Hospital. May 1866 QM duty. August 1866 detached duty at Fort McPherson. Mustered out at Fort Kearney October 1866.

Poteet, Job (Jestin?). Co. B, 64th Va. Mtd. Inf. Enlisted September 1861 at Camp Laney (sp?). Teamster. August 1863 "repairing road." Captured at Cumberland Gap September 9, 1863. (There were thirteen Poteets in the 64th Va. Mtd. Inf. My consultant says that the 64th Va. was raised in the "deepest, darkest part of the redneck kingdom.") POW at Camp Douglas. Age 30. Gray eyes. 5'10" Co. G, 5th US Vols. August 1865 owed sutler $5.00 at Fort Riley. Promoted Sergeant. November 1865 escorting wagon train to Beaver Creek. Mustered out at Fort Kearney October 1866. Invalid pension app 1888. Widow app 1904.

Presgraves, Richard L. Mosby's Regt. Cav. (Partisan Rangers). POW at Point Lookout. Age 25. Blue eyes. 5'10". b. Loudon County. Co. D, 4th US Vols. December 1864 promoted to corporal. May 1865 deserted at Jefferson City, near Omaha. Never caught.

Price, Robert. Co. G, 62nd Va. Mtd. Inf. Nineteen-year old bookkeeper from Virginia. Hazel eyes. 5'4" in CSA records. Deserted CSA service January 1864. POW at Camp Douglas. Age 19. Gray eyes. 5'6". Co. G, 5th US Vols. Deserted August 1865 at Cottonwood. Most of CMSR is missing.

Puples (Pupples, Peeples), John. 12th Va. Cav. POW at Point Lookout. Age 20. Blue eyes. 5'7". b. Wythe County. Had been vaccinated. Co. G, 1st US Vols. Appointed Sergeant May 1864. October 1864 duty on Northern Stockade Line. November 1864 absent sick at Painesville. June 1865 lost cartridge box. September 1865 AWOL. April 1866 escorting paymaster to Fort Leavenworth and Fort Fletcher. May 1866 mustered out at Fort Leavenworth. Widow pension app 1866.

Quesenberry (Quinlan), William. 54th Va. Inf. Captured near Atlanta 1864. POW at Rock Island. Age 24. Dark eyes. 6'0". b. Floyd, Va. Co. C, 3rd US Vols. February 1865 appointed corporal. CMSR devoid of events. Mustered out November 1865. m. Eva. Invalid pension app 1887. Widow pension app 1898. Eight brothers served in the Confederate army.

Quigley (Quigly), William E. Co. A, 26th (Edgar's) Bn. Va. Inf. b. Botetourt County. Enlisted December 1863 at Greenbrier County. Captured June 3, 1864 at Gaines Farm. POW at Point Lookout. Age 26. Gray eyes. 6'5 ½" (sic). Had "fever" 1860. Had alcoholic "fits" but not "horrors" 1861. Had been vaccinated. Illiterate. Co. K, 1st US Vols. September 1864 company cook. September 11, 1865 deserted at Fort Rice. Never caught. 1925 War

Dept. dropped charges and discharged him. There is a 1925 Union pension app on file. It was apparently denied.

Quillin (Quillen), Marion. Co. D, 50th Va. Inf. July 1863 sent to General Hospital No. 9, thence to Chimborazo Hospital, where he spent two months for typhoid. Captured at Spotsylvania May 12, 1864. POW at Point Lookout. Age 18. Blue eyes. 5'10". Co. I, 1st US Vols. May 1864 fined $6 by garrison court-martial. May 1865 deserted at Fort Ridgeley. September 1865 deserted at Fort Snelling. Never caught. Census of 1870, a farmer in Grayson County. Charges dropped and discharge granted 1885. Family requests government grave marker 1932.

Rader, John. Co. B, 8th Va. Cav. Captured at Brooksville, Ky. June 12, 1864. b. Redford, Va. POW at Camp Douglas. Age 42. Hazel eyes. 5'6". Illiterate. Co. H, 6th US Vols. May-June 1865 company cook. July 1865 "home leave" (?). August 1865 deserted at Camp Rankin, near Julesburg, C.T. Took his gun. Owed sutler $3. Never caught.

Ramey, Lewis A. Co. E, 50th Va. Inf. Captured at Gettysburg July 3, 1863. (Same records say he was captured at Spotsylvania CH May 12, 1864.) POW at Point Lookout. Had been vaccinated. Enlisted in Co. A, 1st US Vols. June 1864. Deserted three months later at LaCrosse, Wi., taking his Enfield rifle, 40 rounds of ammunition and all his gear. Never caught. (A mysterious possibility is found in an 1889 Union pension application by "Ramey, Lewis A. [alias] Penic James, unassigned {recruit} 17th Wisconsin Infantry."

Ray (Reay), William H. Co. H, 24th Va. POW at Point Lookout. Age 23. Hazel eyes. 5'11". Co. B, Inf. 4th US Vols. November 1865 QM duty. Mustered out at Fort Leavenworth June 1866.

Redman, John H. Co. C, 64th Va. Mtd. Inf. Enrolled September 1861 at Camp Lane. Sergeant. Captured at Cumberland Gap September 9, 1863. POW at Camp Douglas. Age 24. Blue eyes. 5'6". Co. K, 6th US Vols. August 1865 sick at Julesburg. September-December 1865 at Morrow's Ranch, N.T. Promoted to corporal. November 1865-April 1866 in charge of government hay. June 1866 forage master. July-August 1866 in charge of government corn. Mustered out at Fort Kearney October 1866.

Reed, James W. Enlisted July 1861 Co. K, 6th Va. Cav. Present until wounded at Brandy Station October 1863. POW at Rock Island. Age 24. Hazel eyes. 5'9". b. Clarke Co., Va. Co. B, 3rd US Vols. June 1865 promoted to Sergeant. October 1865 owed Fort Kearney sutler $2.50. Mustered out at Fort Leavenworth November 1865. m. Jennie Hillard. Resided Goresville, Loudoun County. d. March 31, 1905. Buried Monocacy Cemetery, Beallsville, Md. (Michael P. Musick *Sixth Virginia Cavalry*.)

Rees (Reese), Elijah. Co. A, 25th (Heck's) Va. Inf. (Records also show him in Co. G, 5th Va. Inf.) August 1862 promoted to corporal. July 1863 two weeks in Chimborazo Hospital with vulnus sclopeticum (gunshot wound). Court-martialed November 1863 for disrespectful language to Surgeon A. S. Miller. The court was lenient because of "previous good character and 28 days in the guardhouse." (ANVA General Orders.) Captured at Spotsylvania CH May 12, 1864. POW at Point Lookout. Age 25. Gray eyes. 6'6" (sic) b. Marrian, Va. 1856 typhoid. Had been vaccinated. Had piles "sometimes." Scar on left arm from gunshot wound. Co. H, 1st US Vols. September 1864 company cook. Mustered out at Fort Leavenworth November 1865. Invalid pension app 1890.

Rees, Robert F. 5th Bn. Va. Inf. POW at Camp Douglas. Age 17. Hazel eyes. 5'7". Illiterate. b. Washington County, Va. Co. G, 5th US Vols. Deserted at Cottonwood Crossing August 6, 1865, three months after enlisting. Never caught.

Reynolds, James. 64th Va. Mtd. Inf. POW at Camp Douglas. Age 18. Gray eyes. 5'6". Illiterate. b. Lee County, Va. Co. F, 5th US Vols. Deserted at Fort Riley August 1865, owing the sutler $2.50, after serving three months. Never caught.

Reynolds, James C. 64th Va. Mtd. Inf. POW at Camp Douglas. Age 22. Blue eyes. 5'9". b. Floyd, Ga. Enlisted March 1865. Co. H, 6th US Vols. AWOL July 1865. November 1865-February 1866 detached service at St. Mary's, D.T. March-June 1866 in hospital at Fort Laramie. August

1866 QM duties. September 1866 duty as teamster. Mustered out at Fort Kearney October 1866.

Riffle (Riffel), Isaac C. 62nd Va. Mtd. Inf. While in 1st Va. Rangers captured at Braxton County, Va. February 19, 1862 and exchanged at Vicksburg. Captured September 1863 at Lafayette, Ga. Captured by 36th Ohio at Braxton County, as a guerilla. (Record is confusing.) POW at Rock Island. Age 34. Hazel eyes. 5'11". Illiterate. b. Lewis, Va. Co. K, 2nd US Vols. May-June 1865 to garrison post at Running Turkey, Ks. (Probably near Galva, Ks. on the Santa Fé Trail.) September 1865 escort wagons to Indian Corn Mission. Mustered out at Fort Leavenworth November 1865. Invalid pension app 1890. Minor app 1905. Widow app 1910. d. January 1904 at Orlando, W.Va.

Riggs, William H. Co. H, 54th Va. Inf. Enlisted at Rocky Gap August 1862. Captured at Atlanta July 1864. POW at Camp Douglas. Age 18. Blue eyes. 5'8". Illiterate. b. Stokes, N.C. Co. G, 5th US Vols. October 1865 guarding mail station at American Ranch, C.T. May-August 1866 teamster duty in C.T. Deserted September 10, 1866. Never caught. (d. May 26, 1911, Omaha, Ne. This is probably 1st Lieut. William H. Riggs, Co. A, 12th W.Va. Infantry, buried at Forest Lawn Memorial Park, Omaha, not the man of the 5th US Volunteers).

Roach (Roche), Alexander T. Co. G, 41st Va. Inf. Enlisted Petersburg March 1862. Paid $50 bounty. AWOL October-December 1862. Captured May 21, 1864 near

Mt. Carmel Church during the North Anna Campaign. POW at Point Lookout. Age 18. Blue eyes. 5'7". Illiterate. Had been vaccinated. Had measles 1855. b. Prince George County, Va. Co. K, 1st US Vols. Promoted lance corporal. "Good character." March 5, 1865. d. of scurvy Fort Rice. Re-buried at Custer National Cemetery site 190. Laundress Julia Roach is in site 1242.

Roberts, Thomas. Co. C, 44th Va. Inf. May 1863 in hospital No. 9, Richmond. Captured at Spotsylvania May 30, 1864. (Other records say at Wilderness May 12, 1864.) POW at Point Lookout. Age 35. Blue eyes. 5'9". b. Lancashire, England. Illiterate. Had been vaccinated. Had "fever" 1860. Co. I, 1st US Vols. Enlisted May 1864. Deserted at Chicago August 1864. (Other records say Milwaukee.) One record says in jail late August 1864. Rest of record says never caught.

Sally (Salley, Sallie), James K. Co. A, 50th Va. Inf. POW at Point Lookout. Age 18. Blue eyes. 5'6". Illiterate. Had been vaccinated. Once had "fever." Co. I, 1st US Vols. September 1864 teamster. October 1864 and April-June QM duty. July-August 1865 sick at Fort Ridgeley. February 1866 escort to Pond Creek, Ks. Mustered out at Fort Leavenworth May 1866. 1910 in a veterans home with mitral insufficiency (?). Invalid pension app 1888. 1910 widow app. 1912 minor app.

Sampson, George T. 10th Va. Cav. POW at Point Lookout. Age 17. Blue eyes. 5'8". Illiterate. Had measles 1861. Co. D,

1st US Vols. May-July 1864 provost duty at Norfolk. May 14, 1865 died of typhoid fever at Fort Rice. Reburied at Custer National Cemetery site 320. (There is an 1881 invalid pension app for a George T. Sampson. A puzzle.)

Sanders (Saunders), James D. 57th Va. Inf. POW at Point Lookout. Age 37. Hazel eyes. 5'10". b. Bedford, Va. Illiterate. Had typhoid 1861. Co. H, 1st US Vols. August 1864-March 1865 in hospital in St. Louis. Diagnosis "R fever." (Remittent fever, malaria.) May 1865 back on duty. Mustered out Fort Leavenworth November 1865. Invalid pension app 1887. Undated widow app.

Sarber (Sarver), Barney. 54th Va. Inf. POW at Camp Douglas. Age 25. Hazel eyes. 5'6". Illiterate. Co. F, 5th US Vols. June 1866 teamster duty. Mustered out at Fort Kearney October 1866.

Saxton (Sexton), Benjamin F. Co. E, 64th Va. Inf. POW at Camp Douglas. Age 21. Hazel eyes. 5'6". Illiterate. b. Scott, Va. Co. K, 5th US Vols. December 1865-January 1866 mail carrier. April 1866 company cook. May 1866 deserted at Fort Lyon. Never caught.

Saxton (Sexton), Robert. Co. E. 64th Va. Mtd. Inf. POW at Camp Douglas. Age 23. Hazel eyes. 5'5". b. Scott, Va. Illiterate. Co. K, 5th US Vols. July 1865 escorting government herd to Little Creek. October 1865-March 1866 company cook. April-May 1866 teamster duty. June 1866 driving wagon to Pond Creek Station. July-August 1866 QM duty. Mustered out at Fort

Leavenworth November 1866. 1891 invalid pension app.

Schools, Leonard. Cos. A & D. 55th Va. Inf. POW at Point Lookout. Age 40. Gray eyes. 5'11". Illiterate. Had pneumonia 1863. Had delirium tremens three times. Head scalded as a child. Had been vaccinated. Co. H, 1st US Vols. June-October 1865 sent from Fort Rice to hospital at St. Louis with scurvy. Deserted from hospital November 1865. Never caught. Charges dropped in 1925 and discharge issued.

Scott, Charles G. 51st Va. Inf. POW at Point Lookout. Age 20. Blue eyes. 5'7". b. Washington, Va. Illiterate. Co. B, 4th US Vols. December 1865 police duty. April-May 1866 QM duty. Mustered out June 1866 at Fort Leavenworth. Invalid pension app 1890. d. October 1917 at Big Stone Gap, Va. Widow app 1918.

Seacrist (Secrist), Martin V. B. 42nd Va. Inf. POW at Point Lookout. Age 23. Hazel eyes. 5'9". Had been vaccinated. Co. K, 1st US Vols. Sgt. May-June 1865 carpenter. Mustered out at Fort Leavenworth November 1865. In 1870 in Rulo, Nebraska, m. to Anna. (Rulo is in the extreme southeast corner of Nebraska.)

Shankel, George Luther. Co. H, 48th Va. Inf. POW at Point Lookout. Age 22. Light eyes. 5'9". Wheelwright. Illiterate. Had been vaccinated. Measles 1863. Scar right leg. Co. B, 1st US Vols. May-June 1865 herder. Mustered out at Fort Leavenworth November 1865. d. 1906.

Shanks, John T. was the only galvanized Confederate to become a commissioned officer in a Union unit. His CSA records show him as a private in Co. A, 14th Kentucky Cavalry, of Gen. Morgan's raiders, captured at Buffington, Ohio, July 19, 1863, and confined at Camp Douglas. His place of residence: Nacogdoches, Texas. Black eyes. 5'11". "Released by order of the President Dec. 5, 1864." His Union CMSR begins with "Promoted from civilian life . . . Date of commission Apr. 21/65." He was mustered into the 6th US Volunteers May 2, 1865, as a captain. June 1865 escort to Fort Laramie. July 1865 at Camp Rankin, C.T. February 1866 commanding troops between Forts Casper and Laramie. February 1866 absent sick from wounds. May 1866 commanding HQ at Fort Marshall, D.T. August 1866 at Bridger's Ferry, D.T. September 1866 ordered to report to Col. Maynadier. October 1866 mustered out. Dee Brown narrates a possible scandal involving a prisoner shot at close range and pre-war malfeasance.

Shaver, Solomon. 10th Va. Cav. POW at Point Lookout. Age 23. Blue eyes. 5'7". Illiterate. b. Pendleton, Va. Saber scar on head. General health good. Co. D, 1st US Vols. Died at Fort Rice October 30, 1864 of chronic diarrhea. "Nearly always excused by surgeon so but of little service as a soldier." Reburied at site 421, Custer Battlefield National Cemetery.

Shinault, James. Co. G, 63rd (McMahon's) Va. Inf. POW at Rock Island. Age 20. Gray eyes. 5'8". Illiterate. b.

Wythe, Va. Co. H, 3rd US Vols. May 1865 company cook. Mustered out at Fort Leavenworth November 1865, owing $2.90 for destroying the property of John Mattis. Invalid pension app 1881. d. October, 13, 1924 Max, Va. (The 1904 gazetteer published by the US Geological Survey lists Max as a "post village in Carroll County.") Buried at Blue Ridge Baptist Church Cemetery, Carroll County.

Shoemaker, Henry. 64th Va. Mtd. Inf. POW at Camp Douglas. Age 23. Hazel eyes. 5'4". b. Connoway, Va. Co. K, 6th US Vols. April 1865 company cook. July 1865-February 1866 duty as teamster, with January at Cottonwood, and some herder duty. March 1866 absent attending a court-martial at Fort Kearney. Mustered out at Fort Kearney October 1866. Invalid pension app 1891. d. May 1912 at Baxter, Ky. Widow pension app 1916.

Shope, John L. 19th Va. Inf. (1st Va. Arty ?). POW at Point Lookout. Age 23. Blue eyes. 5'7". b. Albemarle. Illiterate. Had been vaccinated. Had measles 1862. Co. D, 1st US Vols. May-August 1865 company cook. September 1865 company baker. Mustered out at Fort Leavenworth November 1865. Requests replacement discharge in 1889. In 1870 census with wife Mary.

Short, Thomas. Co. K, 8th Va. Cav. Captured November 1863 at Floyd County, Ky., "a Confederate deserter . . . home within Federal lines, an especially bad guerrilla and thief." POW at Rock Island. Age 31. Blue eyes. 6'0". b. Wayne, Va. Co. A, 3rd US Vols. May-June 1865 guarding

"M. station, O.C.M.R." (This might be Monument Station on a stage coach route.) July 1865 QM duty. Mustered out at Fort Leavenworth November 1865. Invalid pension app 1890.

Shorter, William H. 47th Va. Cav. POW at Point Lookout. Age 21. Gray eyes. 6'0". b. Rockridge, Va. Co. D, 4th US Vols. Mustered out at Fort Leavenworth June 1866. Invalid pension app 1887. m. Julia Owens 1867.

Skelton, Columbus. Co. K, 10th Va. Inf. April 1862 re-enlisted and received bounty. June 1862 captured and paroled. AWOL November 1862. February 1863 on duty. Captured at Gettysburg July 3, 1863. (Other records say July 4 and 5.) POW at Point Lookout. Age 25. Blue eyes. 5'8". Had typhoid 1862 and smallpox 1863. Co. G, 1st US Vols. Appointed lance Sergeant. "Good character." Died January 8, 1865 at Fort Rice of chronic diarrhea. Reburied at Custer National Cemetery site 328.

Smith, Asa W. Co. L, 10th Va. Inf. Captured at Culp's Hill, Gettysburg July 3, 1863. POW at Point Lookout. Age 28. Brown eyes 5'8". Illiterate. Had typhoid 1863. "Slight" diarrhea. Fractured arm 1863. Drinks "sometimes." Co. G, 1st US Vols. October 1864 on Northern Stockade Line. December 1864 company cook. May 1865 on duty as drummer. Mustered out at Fort Leavenworth May 1865. Invalid pension app 1892. d. April 1914 Madison County, Va.

Smith, Jacob B. Co. E, 54th Va. Missing since retreat from Tullahoma July 6, 1863. Captured at Elk River, Tn. July

1863. POW at Camp Douglas. Age 28. Blue eyes. 5'9". b. Greenbrier, Va. Co. I, 5th US Vols. July 1865 escorting train to Fort Larned. November 1865 deserted near Fort Kearney. Never caught.

Smith, Levi P. Co. D, 31st Va. Inf. June 1863 in hospital at Jordan Springs, Va. Worked many months as shoemaker. Paid $4.90 for 14 pairs of shoes. November 1863-January 1864 Chimborazo Hospital with chronic diarrhea. Captured at Spotsylvania CH. POW at Point Lookout. Age 26. Blue eyes. 5'4". b. Barber, Va. Illiterate. Co. D, 4th US Vols. Promoted Sgt. January 1865, deserted a few days later at Norfolk. Never caught.

Smith, Robert Asbury. Co. G, 63rd (McMahon's) Va. Inf. September 1863 AWOL one month. Charged $17.70 "lost ordnance" (musket?). Captured May 1864 at Resaca, Ga. POW at Alton. Age 19. Blue eyes. 5'8". Co. B, 5th US Vols. Deserted August 1865. Site of desertion variously described as Long Creek, Clifton, and Fort Riley, all Ks. Never caught.

Smith, Robert E. He enlisted as a Sgt. in Co. A, 11th Texas Cavalry at Camp Reeves, Tx. He was captured at Sevierville, Tn. June 27, 1864. Sent first to Camp Chase, then sick to hospital, then to Rock Island. POW at Rock Island. Age 38. Gray eyes. 5'10". b. Falls, Tx. Co. H, 3rd US Vols. June 1865 detached duty at Murray's Ranch. Mustered out at Fort Leavenworth November 1865.

Smith, William H. Co. H, 52nd Va. Inf. Conscript. Wounded at Gaines Mill June 27, 1862. Captured at Gettysburg July 3, 1863. POW at Point Lookout. Age 22. Gray eyes. 5'9". Illiterate. Co. G, 1st US Vols. October 1864 Northern Stockade Line. Company cook December 1864-January 1865, April 1865, and July-August 1865. June 1865 post fifer. October-November 1865 deserted. Site of desertion variously described as Indianola, Fort Leavenworth, and on the march from Leavenworth to Fort Fletcher. Never caught.

Smith, William H. . 52nd Va. Inf. POW at Rock Island. Age 20. Hazel eyes. 5'11". Illiterate. b. Shelby, Al. Co. D, 3rd US Vols. April 1865 "herding government stock." May 1865 teamster duty. June-August 1865 herder. September 1865 detached duty at Post Cottonwood. Mustered out at Fort Leavenworth November 1865.

Snodgrass, Samuel R. 25th Va. Cav. POW at Rock Island. Age 27. Gray eyes. 5'8". b. Lee, Va. Co. D, 3rd US Vols. Sick at Fort Leavenworth hospital March-June 1865. July 1865 escorting supply train to "the first two stations east of Post Cottonwood." Mustered out at Fort Leavenworth November 1865. Invalid pension app 1883.

Southall, Luther T. Co. C, 44th Va. Inf. POW at Point Lookout. Age 21. Blue eyes. 5'9". Had "R. fever" (remittent fever?, rheumatic fever?) 1861, 1862, and 1863. Had been vaccinated. Co. C, 1st US Vols. May 1864 appointed Sergeantt. September 1865 in arrest. November 1865 reduced to the ranks. Mustered out at Fort Leavenworth November 1865. Invalid pension app 1889. d. Baltimore 1917. Widow app 1917.

Southward, Larkin. 47th Va. Inf. POW at Point Lookout. Age 24. Blue eyes. 6'1". Illiterate. Scar left leg from gunshot wound. Had been vaccinated. Co. E, 1st US Vols. September 1865 deserted at Fort Rice, taking $54.58 of "ordnance stores." Never caught.

Sowers, George W. 54th Va. Inf. POW at Rock Island. Age 21. Hazel eyes. 5'10". Co. K, 3rd US Vols. April 1865 lost haversack, charged 65 cents. May-June 1865 detached duty at Horse Shoe, D.T. November 1865 company cook. Mustered out at Fort Leavenworth owing $2.90 for damaging the property of John Mattis. Invalid pension app 1891.

Spence, Burwell. Co. G, 54th Va. Inf. Enlisted September 1861 at Carroll County, Va. Sick in Emory Hospital 1862. Missing on retreat from Missionary Ridge November 26, 1863. Captured at Ringgold November 27, 1863. POW at Rock Island. Age 26. Blue eyes. 5'10". b. Patrick, Va. Co. K, 3rd US Vols. February 1865 promoted to corporal. May-June 1865 duty at "Fort Mackey." Mustered out at Fort Leavenworth November 1865, owing $3.19 for damaging the property of John Mattis. 1885 in Archuleta County, Co. Invalid pension app 1909. d. 1909 at Gunnison, Co. Buried December 14, 1909, Gunnison City Cemetery, Block 50, Lot 10. Widow app 1913.

Sperry, John P. 41ˢᵗ Va. Inf. POW at Point Lookout. Age 20. Blue eyes. 5'5". Had been vaccinated. Co. H, 1ˢᵗ US Vols. September 1865 sent downriver from Fort Rice to hospital at Sioux City. October 1865 discharged at Sioux City. Disability app 1887. d. October 19, 1923 at Erick, Ok.

Steel, George W. Co. F, 41ˢᵗ Va. Cav. Captured at Charleston, W.Va. October 1863. POW at Rock Island. Age 23. Gray eyes. 5'11". b. Hamilton, Oh. Co. D, 3ʳᵈ US Vols. March-June sick at Indiana House, Topeka, Ks. August 1865 at Gillman's Station, N.T. Mustered out at Fort Leaven-worth November 1865. In 1880 census married to Lututia.

Stidham, Andrew Jackson. 64ᵗʰ Va. Mtd. Inf. Enlisted August 1862 Wise County Va. Captured September 1863 Cumberland Gap. POW at Camp Douglas. Age 20. Blue eyes. 5'6". Illiterate. Co. K, 5ᵗʰ US Vols. June 1866 driving wagons to Pond Creek station. Deserted at Fort Lyon C.T. July 1866. Never captured.

Stidham, Samuel. 64ᵗʰ Va. Mtd. Inf. Enlisted at Gray's Farm Va. September 1862. Captured September 1863 at Cumberland Gap. POW at Camp Douglas. Age 21. Blue eyes. 5'5". Illiterate. Co. K, 5ᵗʰ US Vols. July 1865 escorting government herd to Little Creek. August-September company cook. November 1865 escorting wagons to Beaver Creek. June 1866 driving wagons to Pond Creek. Mustered out November 1866. Invalid pension app 1890. d. in Ohio July 1925. Widow app

1931. (It appears the Stidham brothers parted ways on whether to desert.)

Stogdall (Stogdale), George W. Co. A, 52ⁿᵈ Va. Inf. POW at Point Lookout. Age 22. Gray eyes. 6'1". Co. A, 4ᵗʰ US Vols. May-August in Benton Barracks Hospital, St. Louis, with gonorrhea. Discharged September 1865 as too disabled for duty. Invalid pension app 1895. Widow pension app 1910. Wife Margaret.

Stokes, Collins (Colin). Co. K, 38ᵗʰ (Pittsylvania) Va. Inf. October 1861 at home, time expired. March 1863 in Chimborazo Hospital with pneumonia. Captured July 3, 1863 at Gettysburg. In Union hospital at Gettysburg with gunshot wound right breast. Late July 1863 in Union hospital at Baltimore with wound "right lung." "Condition tolerable good . . . spat blood five days." Treated with tonics, stimulants, and simple dressings. Paroled August 1863. November 1863 in Confederate hospital, Danville, Va. with gunshot wound. April 1864 brief stay at Hospital No. 9, Richmond. Captured at Petersburg May 10, 1864. POW at Point Lookout. Age 27. Dark eyes. 5'7". History of typhoid. Had been vaccinated. Old chest wound noted. Illiterate. Co. K, 1ˢᵗ US Vols. November 1864 duty as baker. October 1865 sent from Fort Rice to Fort Leavenworth, where he mustered out November 1865. Invalid pension app 1900. d. January 6, 1931 at Farmville, Va. Buried Westview Cemetery. Wife Florence.

Stout, John. Co. D, 20th Va. Cav. Deserted CSA service July 1863. Arrested August 24, 1863 in Bath County, Va. POW at Camp Chase. (Other records say Rock Island.) Age 19, Hazel eyes. 5'5". Illiterate. Co. K, 2nd US Vols. May-June 1865 garrison duty at Running Turkey, Ks. September,1865 escort to (illegible). Mustered out November 1865 at Fort Leavenworth. Invalid pension app November 1892.

Stover, Jacob M. 18th Va. Cav. POW at Point Lookout. Age 21. Hazel eyes. 5'5". Illiterate. Co. E, 4th US Vols. Deserted at Sioux City June 1865. Captured at Fort Sully, court-martialed and sentenced to hard labor. Confined January-May 1866 then discharged. Disability app 1884. d. December 18, 1915, Madison, Va.

Sutphin, Asa L. Co. D, 54th Va. Inf. From Floyd County. Enlisted October 1861. Captured May 1864 Cassville, Ga. POW at Rock Island. Age 27 (22). Gray eyes. 5'6". Illiterate. Co. C, 3rd US Vols. May-June 1865 detached service. Mustered out at Fort Leavenworth November 1865. (The 1860 census shows Asa age 14, son of Christopher and Susan Sutphin. Asa was born January 25, 1848 and died November 30 1931 in Boone County, In. He married Vinetta Goad in 1863. (They had sixteen children.) In 1893 his mother filed for a pension.

Sutphin, Harrison. Co. D, 54th Va. Inf. Born Floyd County, April 16, 1846, son of Riley S. Sutphin and Mary Houchins Sutphin. POW at Rock Island. Age 18. Gray eyes. 5'10". Illiterate. Co. C, 3rd US Vols. May-June 1865 detached service. August 1865 cutting hay. Mustered out at Fort Leavenworth November 1865. Invalid pension app 1890. Widow app 1917.

Sutphin, Lafayette. Co. D, 54th Va. Inf. 16-year old farm laborer born August 5, 1844, same parents as Harrison Sutphin. Sick October 1863 at Kingston, Ga. Captured May 1864 at Cassville, Ga. POW at Rock Island. Age 20. Hazel eyes. 5'11". Able to write his name. Co. C, 3rd US Vols. Promoted to corporal February 1865. Mustered out at Fort Leavenworth November 1865 owing $3.18 for damaging property of John Mattis. Invalid pension app 1890. Died November 9, 1917, buried at Nibletts Bluff Cemetery, Vinton, La. Widow pension app 1916 (!).

Sutphin, Madison C. Co. G, 54th Va. Inf. Enlisted March 1862 at Russell County, Va. December 1863 arrested for desertion. Issued clothing April 1864. Captured May 1864 at Dalton, Ga. POW at Camp Morton. Age 22. Brown eyes. 5'9". Illiterate. Co. C, 6th US Vols in 1865. Conflicting records. Deserted August 1865. Died of typhoid June 1865. Both at Fort Leavenworth. The pension index has no one by this name. m. Sara Bolt 1861.

Sweeny, William. 24th Va. Cav. He was captured at Spotsylvania CH May 1864 and sent to Point Lookout. Co. F, 1st US Vols. August 1864 with the drum corps at Milwaukee. February 1865 at Fort Rice. November 1865 deserted on the march from Fort Leavenworth to Fort Fletcher. Never caught. In 1913 asked the War

Department for a honorable discharge, which was granted. Soon after this, he received an invalid pension (also used the alias of Charles A. Sherman). He died at Mount Washington, Mo. June 2, 1921. In 1922 his widow got a pension. Buried Mount Saint Mary's Cemetery, Kansas City, Jackson County, Missouri.

Sweet, John Walker. Co. H, 25th (Heck's) Va. Inf. Residence Rockbridge Co. Va. Enlisted May 21, 1861. Detailed as wagoner September 1861. AWOL May 1862. Detailed as teamster September 1862 and June 1863. Furloughed January 1864. Captured May 5, 1864 at the Wilderness. POW at Point Lookout. Age 30. Gray eyes. 6'0". Illiterate. Had been vaccinated. Had measles. Co. E, 1st US Vols. May 1865 on detached service en route to Fort Sully. October 1865 detached service, not specified. Mustered out at Fort Leavenworth November 1865.

Taylor, George W. Co. A, 55th Va. Inf. Enlisted July 1861. April 1862 sick in hospital at Milford. July 14, 1863 captured at Falling Waters. Died of disease December 27, 1864 (???) . A three-page nearly illegible letter is in his CSA CMSR. Three men of this name are listed in the US Volunteers: Co. K, 5th US Vols, Co. F, 1st US Vols, and Co. G, 2nd US Vols. He is probably the man in the 1st US Vols. POW at Point Lookout. Age 26. Blue eyes. 5'8". Had chronic diarrhea in 1863. Had been vaccinated. Deserted July 1864 at Elizabeth City, taking his Enfield rifle. Virginia pension app 1918. Augusta County.

Thompson, Charles Edward. Co. A, 12th Va. Cav. Paid $12 per month for his horse. Captured May 12, 1863 at Loudon County. (Other records say Winchester, Purcellville, and Middleburg.) POW at Point Lookout. Co. I, 1st US Vols. Deserted August 1, 1864 at Pasquotank, N.C., after serving five months. Records contain an undated memo from the Robert E. Lee Camp Soldier's Home. (The "Old Soldiers Home" operated 1884-1914 in Richmond.)

Thompson, David Fleming. Co. F, 45th Va. Inf. Enlisted May 1861 at Wytheville, Va. Sick July 1861. In hospital at Richmond, Va. February 1862. Captured September 1864 at Winchester. Died in 1907. POW at Point Lookout. Age 23. Blue eyes. 5'11". Co. C, 4th US Vols. Deserted at Norfolk January 1865 after three months of service.

Thompson, Samuel. Co. B, 15th Va. Cav. (A Samuel Thompson served in Co. E, 51st Va. Inf.) Enlisted July 1863 at Fredericksburg. Captured at Falmouth April 1864. Two men by this name: Co. K, 1st US Vols, and Co. B, 2nd US Vols. The 1st US Vols soldier was a POW at Point Lookout. Age 21. Blue eyes. 6'1". Had never been vaccinated. July 1864 provost duty at Norfolk. September 1864 deserted at Sioux City and captured three weeks later at Fort Randall. Whilst being sent to his regiment at Fort Rice, on board the steamer *Effie Dean*, he deserted again. At his general court-martial one of the charges was that he threatened to kill his officers. He was sentenced to lose two months pay. (The whole story is complex.) He was mustered out with his regiment and in 1890 applied for a disability pension.

Toman, William H. R. 25th Va. Inf. POW at Point Lookout. Age 18. Blue eyes. 6'0". Had typhoid 1862. Drinks "sometimes." Ax scar left foot. Co. H, 1st US Vols. October 1865 escorting wagons from Fort Rice to Fort Leavenworth. Mustered out November 1865 at Fort Leavenworth. Invalid pension app 1884. d. July 1917 at Aquia, Va. Widow app 1917.

Travis, James. 64th Va. Mtd. Inf. POW at Camp Douglas. Age 20. Gray eyes. 5'10". Co. G, 5th US Vols. August 1865 at Fort Riley, owing $2.50 to the sutler. February 1866 cutting wood at (illegible). March 1866 deserted at Fort Wardwell, C.T., owing $28 for his musket. Never caught.

Trayler (Traylor), Henry Augustus. Co. H, 44th Bn. Va. Inf. Enlisted at Amelia CH. September 1862 in hospital at Farmville. June 1863 in hospital No. 11 at Richmond. July 1863 in Chimborazo Hospital with "debility." September 1864 in hospital at Charlottesville with rheumatism. Captured at Strasburg September 1864. Sent to Point Lookout. Co. D, 4th US Vols. CMSR not in Fold3. Invalid pension app 1898. Died December 8, 1903. Buried Oakwood Cemetery, Richmond.

Tyson, John W. Co. A, 7th Va. Inf. Enlisted October 1862 at Culpeper CH. In Chimborazo hospital May 1864. Captured July 3 at Gettysburg. POW at Point Lookout.

Age 18. Blue eyes. 6'0". Illiterate. Had been vaccinated. Tinsmith. Co. G, 1st US Vols. October 1864 on Northern Stockade Line. February 1865 in arrest. April 1866 confined at Fort Snelling awaiting court-martial. June 1865 back on duty. October 1865 deserted on the march from Fort Leavenworth to Fort Fletcher. Never caught. January1866 married Rebecca Grantham at Leavenworth, Ks. perhaps under the alias of John W. James. 1889 War Dept. dropped charges and issued a discharge. Invalid pension app 1890. Died 1912 at Dade County, Mo. Widow pension app.

Vaden, James Munroe. Co. E, 4th Va. Inf. Enlisted Princeton October 1863. Captured Spotsylvania CH May 1864. POW at Point Lookout. Age 18. Blue eyes. 5'10". Had been vaccinated. Cos. A and F, 1st US Vols. In 1865: February QM duty; March stable duty; April teamster; May guard hay barn; June-August QM duty. October-December teamster. In 1866: January at Fort Riley; February at Pond Creek station; April-May at Fort Fletcher. Mustered out while still at Fort Fletcher. 1889 discharge certificate issued. Invalid pension app 1885. d. Ironto, Va. October 15, 1924. Widow app 1924. Buried in Reesedale Cemetery, Ironto, Montgomery County. Second wife, Hattie Alls, lived until 1940. His gravestone is almost displaced by a large tree.

Vaughn, Alexander. Co. C, 3rd (Archer's) Bn. Va. Res. Enlisted at Kinston, N.C. April 1863. A substitute. "Deserted July 4, 1863 at Gettysburg." "Exchanged December

1863." (Exchanged?) POW at Point Lookout. Age 16. Hazel eyes. 5'7". Had been vaccinated. Intermittent fever 1864. Co. F, 1st US Vols. In 1865: May guarding hay train; August drummer; October teamster; December log detail. Mustered out at Fort Leavenworth May 1866.

Viehmeyer (Vieghmeyer, Viehmeyster, Viemyer), Wilhelm (William). Co. A, 10th Va. Cav. Enlisted February 1862 at Richmond, as a substitute. April 1862 in Hospital No. 18, Richmond. May 1862 at Camp Winder. (A Wilhelm Viahmeir served in the 1st La. Zouaves.) b. Bielsfield, Germany. Arrived 1859 from Bremen. Shoemaker. Captured at Manassas Gap July 23, 1863. POW at Point Lookout. Age 20. Gray eyes. 5'4". Chills and fever every year since a boy. Had been vaccinated. Co. B, 1st US Vols. February 1865 herder at Cannon Ball River. September 1865 orderly for post adjutant. Mustered out at Fort Leavenworth November 1865. In 1902 wife in Erie, Pa. (?)

Waid (Wade), Luther R. Co. I, 52nd Va. Inf. 22-year old farmer of Augusta Co. Enlisted July 1861. AWOL February 1862, June 1862, and November 1862. Hospitalized with rheumatism Staunton, Va. February 1863. Captured July 1863 at Williamsport, Md. POW at Point Lookout. Age 26. Blue eyes. 5'8". Blacksmith. Had been vaccinated. Had measles 1860. Co. B, 1st US Vols. August-November hospital at Benton Barracks, Mo. December 1864-October 1865 in Marine Hospital,

St. Louis. Phthisis pulmonaris. (tuberculosis of the lung). "Most probably developed since enlistment." He requested discharge. Died May 1867 in "County Poor House." No record of pension application.

Watts, Marion. Co. B, 34th Bn. Va. Cav. Enlisted April 1862 at Logan County. January 1863 detached service. July 3 (other records say July 4), 1863 captured at Gettysburg. POW at Point Lookout. Age 19, Blue eyes. 5'9". Co. F, 1st US Vols. In hospital at Fort Ridgely, Mn. from October 1864 to May 1865. November 1865 escorting wagons from Fort Fletcher to Monument Station, Ks. April 1866 escorting wagons to Fort Leavenworth, where he was mustered out in May. Invalid pension app 1889. d. February 23, 1920 near East Lynn, Wayne County, W.Va., alias Francis M. Watts. Buried Osburn Cemetery. Government issue tombstone reads "Co. F, 1st Regt. US Vol. Inf." Widow Martha Jane Fry app 1920.

Whanger, David W. Co. D, 26th (Edgar's) Bn. Va. Inf. POW at Rock Island. Age 28. Gray eyes. 6'2". Co. K, 3rd US Vols. February 1865 appointed corporal. May 1865 at Platte Bridge, D.T. Mustered out November 1865 at Fort Leavenworth, owing $3.19 for damaging the property of John Mattis. Widow app 1878.

Whitesell (Whitsel), Joseph S. Co. E, 54th Va. Inf. Enlisted at Christiansburg, Va. September 1861. Deserted September 1863, taking his gun. Captured at Chickamauga November 26, 1863. POW at Rock Island. Age 24. Blue eyes, 5'4" (or 5'9"). Pre-war carpenter. Co.

G, 2ⁿᵈ US Vols. April-July 1865 duty as carpenter. Mustered out at Fort Leavenworth November 1865.

Whittaker, George. Co. E, 47ᵗʰ Va. Inf. Captured Gettysburg July 3, 1863. POW at Point Lookout. Age 19. Gray eyes. 5'8". Illiterate. b. Caroline, Va. Co. C, 4ᵗʰ US Vols. CMSR has few entries. Mustered out at Fort Leavenworth July 1866. Widow app 1891.

Whittaker (Wittico), Henry. 47ᵗʰ Va. Inf. (Same data as George.) Age 23. Gray eyes. 5'9". Illiterate . Co. C, 4ᵗʰ US Vols. March 1865 arrested in Norfolk for stealing commissary whiskey and "drawing a weapon on a Negro." One month at Hard Labor Camp, working on the streets, with a 30-pound ball and chain. He had a visit from George. Rest of CMSR is just "present for duty." Mustered out at Fort Leavenworth July 1866.

Whittiker, Edward H. 1ˢᵗ Va. Cav. POW at Rock Island. Age 23. Light eyes. 5'11". Clerk. b. Cecil, Md. Co. B, 2ⁿᵈ US Vols. March 1865 post sergeant major at Fort Zarah. Mustered out at Fort Leavenworth November 1865.

Williams, Isaac. Co. C, 64ᵗʰ Va. Mtd. Inf. Enlisted February 1863. Captured September 1863 at Cumberland Gap. POW at Camp Douglas. Age 20. Blue eyes. 5'10". b. Scott. Va. Illiterate. Co. G, 5ᵗʰ US Vols. April 1865 owed Fort Riley sutler $2.50. May-September 1865 company cook. June 1866 QM duty. August 1866 at Fort McPherson, N.T. Mustered out at Fort Kearney October 1866, owing $8.60 for lost drum. Invalid pension app 1890. d. 1892. Buried Hollywood Cemetery, Richmond, Va., Section 23, lot 71.

Williams, John. Co. C, 64th Va. Mtd. Inf. Enlisted February 1863 at Holston Spring. Deserted May 1863. Captured at Cumberland Gap September 9, 1865. POW at Camp Douglas (Illinois). Age 22. Black eyes. 5'8". "Claims to have been loyal and was conscripted." March 1866 deserted at Camp Douglas, U.T. (Utah), taking his Enfield rifle and all gear. Never caught. Three men with that name served in the US Vols.: Co. K, 3rd US Vols; Co. A, 6th US Vols; Co. K, 6th US Vols. The soldier from Co. A, 6th US Vols seems most likely to be the Utah deserter.

Williams, John F. 2nd US Vols. Assistant surgeon. (It's not clear why he is on this list. He was not galvanized). Age 25. May-September 1865 at Fort Dodge. April 1865 Gen. Dodge ordered the commissary to provide Williams with whatever was needed to combat scurvy. Mustered out at Fort Leavenworth November 1865. Prior service as musician in the 15th Illinois Cavalry and in the 53rd Illinois Infantry. Disability pension app 1900. d. July 6, 1927, Evansville, Il.

Williams, John P. Co. K, 5th US Vols. POW at Camp Douglas. Age 20. Hazel eyes. 5'7". b. Cherokee, Al. Illiterate. Deserted August 1865 at Running Turkey, Ks. (See Isaac Riffle.) Never caught.

Willis, Henry Francis. Co. F, 48th Va. Inf. Enlisted June 1861 Washington Co. In hospital August 1861. On furlough

February 1862. In hospital August 1862 (acute diarrhea). Court-martialed December 1863. Captured May 1864 Spotsylvania CH. POW at Point Lookout. Age 25. Blue eyes. 5'8". Illiterate. Had been vaccinated. Told examiner he'd never been sick. Co. K, 1st US Vols. August 1864-April 1865 (eight months!) in hospital at Norfolk. d. May 1865 of rheumatism and diarrhea. His regiment was at Fort Berthold when Willis died at Norfolk.

Wilson, George Alexander. 37th Bn. Va. Cav. POW at Rock Island. Age 24. Hazel eyes. 5'8". Co. K, 3rd US Vols. June 1865 at Platte Bridge, D.T. October 1865 left sick at Fort Laramie to be mustered out. No diagnosis in CMSR. Invalid pension app 1902. d. September 12, 1907 (Other records say September 3.) at Piedmont, S.C. Buried at Rose Hill Cemetery, Piedmont, Greenville, S.C. Gravestone tall, deeply stained.

Wilson, Hezekiah. Co. B, 31st Va. Inf. AWOL November 1862. In hospital April 1863. Captured September 1864 at Fisher's Hill, Va. POW at Point Lookout. Age 29. Blue eyes. 5'7". Illiterate. Co. C, 4th US Vols. In hospital at Norfolk March 1865 to March 1866, with pulmonary tuberculosis, "hereditary." Discharged as totally disabled.

Wilson, James P. Co. I, 48th Va. Inf. Enlisted June 1861. On furlough February 1862. Captured May 1864 at Spotsylvania CH. POW at Point Lookout. Age 22. Gray eyes. 5'8". Had been vaccinated. Health "good." Co. K,

1st US Vols. May 23, 1865 died of scurvy at post hospital, Fort Rice. Reburied at Custer National Cemetery, site 289.

Wilson, John. Co. B, Capt. Archibald Graham's Co. of Va. Light Artillery (Rockbridge Artillery). Enlisted July 1861 near Manassas. $50 bounty. Captured July 5, 1863 near Waterloo, Pa. (Other records say July 3, 1863 at Gettysburg.) POW at Point Lookout. Age 28. Blue eyes. 6'0". Illiterate. b. Rockbridge, Va. Had cholera 1863. Had been vaccinated. At least three John Wilsons served in the US volunteers: Co. E, 1st US Vols; Co. A, 2nd US Vols; 4th US Vols. He is probably of Co. E, 1st US Vols. December 1864-April 1865 company cook. September 1865 deserted at Fort Rice, taking all his gear, plus $100 of QM stores. Captured five days later and confined at Fort Leavenworth. Later returned to Fort Rice without trial and mustered out. 1895 disability pension app.

Wilson, John E. In Confederate service there were eleven men named John E. Wilson and twenty-three named J. E. Wilson. Exact identification seems next to impossible. POW at Alton. Age 26. Gray eyes. 6'1". Illiterate. b. Anderson District, S.C. Co. E, 5th US Vols. Hospital nurse November 1865-January 1866. February 1866 at Camp Collins, C.T. Mustered out at Fort Kearney October 1866.

Wilson, John T. Co. I, 36th Va. Inf. Enlisted January 1863. Captured September 1864 Winchester. POW at Point

Lookout. Three John T. Wilsons appear in the volunteer records: Co. E, 1st US Vols; Co. A, 2nd US Vols; 4th US Vols.

Wolfe (Wolf), Peter F. Co. A, 23rd Bn. Va. Inf. Enlisted April 1862. Captured October 1864 at Winchester, Va. POW at Point Lookout. Age 30. Hazel eyes. 5'10". Illiterate. Co. B, 4th US Vols. December 1864-February 1865 company cook. November 1865-May 1866 QM Dept. Mustered out at Fort Leavenworth June 1866.

Woods (Wood), George W. Co. D, 19th Va. Inf. Enlisted June 1861 at Centerville. Sick at home September-December 1861. Wounded and captured at Williamsburg May 5, 1862. Absent, dates unclear. Captured at Gettysburg July 3, 1863. POW at Point Lookout. Age 25. Blue eyes. 6'0". Illiterate. Had been vaccinated. 1861 had typhoid. Co. C, 1st US Vols. June-July 1864 guard duty at Norfolk. September 1865 deserted at Fort Rice taking his musket. Never caught.

Woods, Stephen (Steaver) C. 25th Va. Cav. (My consultant says, "The 25th Va. Cav. was fully organized . . . a western bushwhacker outfit . . . the only Stephen Woods in Virginia service was in the 64th Va. Mtd. Inf., another boondocks unit . . . he may have been in both.") Co. K, 1st US Vols. Cannot locate CMSR on Fold3.

Yeatts (Yates), Thomas Madeline. Co. B, 21st Va. Inf. Enlisted April 1864 at Pittsylvania (his birthplace). Captured September 1864 Strasburg, Va. POW at Point Lookout. Age 18. Gray eyes. 5'8". Illiterate. Co. D, 4th US Vols.

November 1865 detailed as post orderly. (An illiterate orderly?) Mustered out at Fort Leavenworth June 1866. Requests a replacement certificate, 1889. Invalid pension app 1889. d. July 10, 1910 at Elba, Va. Widow app 1910. Buried Pines Cemetery, Gretna, Pittsylvania County, Va. Gravestone cracked with heavy lichen.

CHAPTER 11
GLEANINGS AND CONCLUSIONS

What can we conclude from the findings in the roster of Virginians who "galvanized" into the blue uniforms of the United States Volunteers? First, any competent statistician or demographer would raise the alarm of sampling error. Can men who were captured represent Confederate soldiers in general? Did men who surrendered lack a willingness to fight to the last bullet, to the last man, to the last inch of ground? Were these cowardly, craven men, insufficiently devoted to The Cause? Or was it merely the much clichéd Fog of War that left one man with his regiment, while another marched off to a Yankee prison? Millennia ago, Ecclesiastes noted that the race is not to the swift, nor the battle to the strong, but that time and chance governeth all things. The question of whether Confederates who surrendered were measurably different from their comrades is probably unanswerable. But what of those who galvanized, compared with those thousands of prisoners who rejected the shelter of a blue uniform?

The records, like all such in the Civil War, were gathered *ad hoc*, to serve the needs of the moment. Each Union prison camp gathered data in a somewhat different manner, thus lumping all the prisons together will surely introduce conclusionary errors. Civil War records were created for the users and not for us, a century and a half later. Each army contained men with a spectrum of motives for joining. Some were eager volunteers, some were conscripted men, and yet others were paid substitutes. Were the latter more eager to surrender and perhaps to galvanize? And how about regional differences, such as those between the more dedicated coastal men and those in the western mountains, who saw nary a slave and were content to work their little scraps of land and insulate themselves from the rages and tantrums of both Carolina fire-eaters and Massachusetts abolitionists?

Teasing all these factors out of the millions of pages of hand-written documents would be a lifetime project for any researcher and the present writer has the ordinary mortal limitations. For all the reasons cited above, any conclusions must apply to the 292 men in this roster, and only to this group. (However, anyone who believes that these conclusions cannot be reasonably extrapolated to Confederate troops in general faces a monumental task.) For the interested reader, here are the Virginia findings.

Camps of Origin

Nearly all the galvanized Virginia men were from five Union prisoner of war camps. Those camps, with the number of men from each, were: Point Lookout (169); Rock Island (63); Camp Douglas (56); Alton (5); and Camp Morton (4). This distribution clearly reflects the usual activities of Virginia troops in the Eastern theatre not the Western one. Nearly every Confederate captured at Gettysburg went to Point Lookout.

Literacy

Most published studies of literacy define it as the ability of a 15-year old to read and understand simple instructions and to write short simple sentences in the most basic vocabulary of his native language. In this study the decision as to literacy uses a much lower standard: the ability to sign one's own name. Those failing this test signed their enlistment papers with an "X" to which was added the words "His Mark." In the records which still contain enlistment papers, 133 white male Confederate enlisted men, most them in their early twenties, were unable to write their own name, yielding a literacy rate of 54 percent. For comparison, the literacy rate in 1860 in Great Britain was 75 percent and, in France, 65 percent. For the United States overall, the rate was 80 percent. For the enlisted ranks in the Confederate armies, the degree of basic literacy was dramatically below the world norm for civilized nations. Placing these figures into a visual concept, consider that when General Pickett's men stepped out of the trees and began the one-mile charge of undying fame that capped the Battle of Gettysburg, 8,000 of his men couldn't even write their own names. (Jumping forward 150 years we find these current rates: World in general 88 percent; Albania 98 percent; Botswana 88 percent; and the United States 99 percent.)

On the subject of extrapolation, two long-term eminent scholars add a deeper perspective. Michael P. Musick notes the Georgia Hussars, whose papers are all signed with an "X." Since this unit of highly social, politically powerful elite men was not likely to be illiterate, they were probably too busy to trouble themselves with such trivia as signing papers. Robert K. Krick, who has also read thousands of original manuscripts, suggests that roughly twenty-five percent of CSA soldiery were illiterate at the "signed with an X" level, with a range of 20 percent to 35 percent. The 47 percent finding in the galvanized men is "not characteristic by any means." Perhaps men whose lack of education foreshadowed a dim future in the post-war South might find that Union service held greater promise.

Smallpox Vaccination

Smallpox appears in the earliest written records. Its ability to kill or disfigure terrified whole populations. The author still has in a desk drawer the yellow vaccination document required of all international travelers. It was not until 1979 that this scourge was eliminated worldwide. The first successful control of smallpox is attributed to English physician Edward Jenner (1749-1823) who noticed that milkmaids had better complexions than the general population. Their exposure to cowpox, a less virulent form of the virus, protected them against the more deadly virus, which produced the skin craters and scars so prominent on millions who had survived an attack. By the time of the Civil War vaccination was well-known. In 1863, Union Army Regulation 1299 advised commanders that "as soon as a recruit joins any regiment . . . he shall be examined by the medical officer and vaccinated when required." But well before 1863, vaccination was widespread. As much as soldiers feared smallpox they also feared vaccination. The crude preparations available in the 1860s often resulted in serious infections and even death.

How common was vaccination among Confederate soldiers? The best medical records from the prison camps are those from Point Lookout. Of the 169 men who galvanized at that facility, seventy-four had recorded prior vaccinations. The Confederate medical department was certainly up to date in medical practice.

Desertion

Desertion is not a popular subject among Civil War aficionados. In the first serious study of the subject, historian Ella Lonn, in her classic 1928 monograph *Desertion during the Civil War*, spent the first chapter apologizing to Civil War veterans and their descendants, for impugning the courage and dedication of any soldier, North or South. Even today re-enactors and book buyers clearly prefer battle analyses and biographies of famous generals over studies of less heroic events.

What facts and figures exist to quantify desertion? E. B. Long, in *The Civil War Day by Day*, addresses the many problems inherent in deriving Civil War statistics and suggests the following: two million men served in the Union armies. The figure for the Confederate forces is 750,000. As of late 1864, 50 percent of all Confederate soldiers were absent from their posts; in the Union armies, the figure was 30 percent. The total number of Union deserters was close to 200,000 (ten percent of all the men who ever served); the equivalent Confederate figure was 104,000 (fourteen percent of all the men who ever served). The bases for these figures are explored in greater detail in the author's *Merciful Lincoln*, pages 47-80. What are the numbers for the galvanized Virginians?

Sixty-nine deserted during their terms of enlistment; twenty-four percent of the galvanized Virginians left with the intent of never returning, a desertion rate more than twice that of Union forces in general. Almost none were caught. We have found no letters or diaries documenting their motivations for departure, leaving us with only speculation. (The Confederacy did not keep accurate records of how many deserted and were never caught.)

Death by Disease

Twenty-seven galvanized Virginians died of disease while in service, nine percent of this population. Death by disease in the Union army overall was eleven percent. For the Confederate armies, the percentage was twenty-two percent. It would seem that galvanized service was slightly healthier than Union service in general and twice as healthy as Confederate service. The most common causes of galvanized death were diarrhea and scurvy.

Death from Hostile Indians

Not a single galvanized Virginian was killed by an Indian. One was wounded. Pvt. John J. Cumby, Company E, 1st US Volunteers, was on outpost in mid-May 1865 near Fort Rice when a musket ball, fired by an Indian, shattered the middle third of his right radius and caused the elbow joint to become fixed and immobile. After four months in a St. Louis hospital he was given a medical discharge. His 1869 pension application would contain the results of many detailed examinations.

Too Sick to Serve

Twenty-six galvanized Virginians were discharged for medical reasons, as too sick to complete their enlistments.. Some went almost directly from the recruiter's office to a hospital and never spent a day in active service. Seventeen cases had no diagnosis noted in the CMSR. Three discharges were for pulmonary tuberculosis and a like number for diarrhea / dysentery. There was one discharge for each of these conditions: cataract, right eye; ulcerated cornea; typhoid fever; and gonorrhea.

Hearts and Minds

Literary giants such as Stephen Crane and his *Red Badge of Courage*, and the several magisterial Civil War novels of Ralph Peters are vivid and convincing portrayals of the motivations of those men long ago, in their tattered gray and blue uniforms. But what do we have of the <u>actual</u> thoughts and feelings of our galvanizing Virginians? Do we have detailed and intimate diaries? Do we have contemporary letters which speak of emotions and motivations? Do we have post-war memoirs, even with *ex post facto* justifications for jumping to the Union side? Sadly, the answer seems to be "no." Since more than half of these Virginians could not even write their own names, such records would be sparse. But even the literate seem to have left us nothing. We can re-create their feelings only as projections of our own feelings. The deepest thoughts of these men will always elude us. "Breathes there the man, with soul so dead . . .

Who never to himself hath said, this is my own, my native land!" Sir Walter Scott's timeless meditation upon personal and national identity seems a perfect entrée into the subject of post-war Galvanized Virginians. Did they return to the South after the war? Did they fear accusations of treason and betrayal? Did they instead flee to the gold mines of Montana and Nevada, or to the rapidly developing and sunny climes of California? A prolonged search of the US Census records might yield some answers, but a quicker answer lies closer at hand: the burial sites of these men. These final resting places are recorded for only a fraction of the men, but they can at least suggest a trend. (They do not include men dying in service, mostly buried in national cemeteries.)

Virginia (25); West Virginia (4); Missouri (3); Kentucky (3); Tennessee (3); Colorado (3); and one each in Nebraska, Oklahoma, Ohio, Louisiana, Illinois, South Carolina, South Dakota, California, Pennsylvania, Oregon, and Minnesota. It's clear that the great majority returned to their home territory.

Conclusions

For a variety of reasons at least 3,000 Confederate soldiers, including our 292 Virginians, chose Union service over prison life. In the Virginia group, they died of disease less often than men still in active service in the rest of the Union and Confederate armies. They deserted far more often than Union forces in general. Although they were part of forces designed to subdue the often war-like Plains Indians, not a single Virginian was killed by a Native American.

An effect of galvanizing, little noted, but certainly present, was a changed view. Until the 1860s, men thought of themselves as living in the North or in the South. They had strong state identities. (Robert E. Lee defined himself as a Virginian, not as an American.) The US Volunteers, looking back to their Eastern origins from their new surroundings, saw the nation differently. The little meadows of the Eastern forests were dwarfed by the endless plains. The Blue Ridge Mountains were now mere hummocks compared with the Rockies. Their previous association with identical men was replaced by comrades of every region and a dozen countries, bound by shared combat, shared labor, and shared struggles against thirst and freezing winds. They became veterans of not just the Union or the Confederacy but veterans of a whole new country, a first step in the long and still-continuing struggle against the bitterness of sectionalism.

Coda

Perhaps the stories of the galvanized Virginians will inspire other writers to study the remaining states and their galvanized alumni: Kentucky (132); North Carolina (421); South Carolina (73); Tennessee (688); Georgia (464); Florida (78); Alabama (564); Mississippi (325); Missouri (78); Arkansas (149); Texas (146); and Louisiana (300).

ROBERT E. DENNEY

Bob's valuable research into the world of Galvanized Yankees is described in the chapter on Sources. In person, this remarkable man had two lives: his military career and his later years. He was never still, always looking for some new way to be creative or productive or helpful.

He began life September 26, 1929, in a small mid-Western town, which he felt to be limiting, stultifying. In 1947, as soon as he graduated from high school, he signed on for a three-year hitch with the US Marine Corps. They sent him to China which was in the throes of a civil war and a famine. He guarded a trainload of food destined for one of the worst areas of famine. But there was hunger everywhere and every mile of track had people anxious to help themselves. In one brawl, he was knifed but saved himself by using his USMC belt, with its heavy bronze buckle. His Marine years included time on Guam.

As soon as he completed his Marine Corps service, he enlisted in the US Army. Just in time for Korea. He spent many months in heavy combat, including perilous commando operations, far behind Communist lines. Fifty years later, his few attempts to describe those actions left him unable to speak, weeping for lost comrades. His Korea service gave him a serious wound and three decorations, the Silver Star, the Bronze Star with Valor clasp, and a Purple Heart. Stateside, he spent time as a drill sergeant and earned a promotion to warrant officer. In 1956, he graduated from the Warrant Officer's Flight School as a helicopter pilot. But he was no ordinary pilot, and was soon active in the development of low-level navigation for helicopters. For his contributions, he was awarded the Army Commendation Medal.

Then came Viet Nam. He often terrified his crew chief by flying his helicopter into very dangerous zones, usually to pickup wounded men. The North Koreans put a bullet through his flight helmet, which filled one eye with fragments of plastic. For his Viet Nam service he was awarded the Distinguished Flying Cross, another Bronze Star (Oak Leaf Cluster), several air medals, and a second Purple Heart. He retired in 1967 with the rank of major.

Bob settled in northern Virginia and enrolled in Strayer College, where he earned both a bachelor's and a master's degrees in computer science. He wore his Strayer

ring proudly. His self-motivation and work standards probably meant more than a Harvard ring, earned with daddy's
money and lots of elitist conviviality. He was always doing
something for somebody, just like his idol, Abraham Lincoln.
Bob often spoke of his "girl friends." I soon learned that these
were elderly ladies for whom he built wheelchair ramps and
visited just to socialize. Many were diabetic. He would bring
one donut and they would split it. Each got a taste of shared
sweetness, without the need for another shot of insulin. (Bob,
too, was diabetic.) He was always bestowing pâté or Brunswick Stew on friends. When Beverly and I moved to Virginia
we drove across the country in early January, through a series
of blizzards. He calculated our arrival time and, the day
before, talked his way into our locked and gated apartment
building and persuaded the security guard to let him into our
apartment, where he left pasta, spaghetti sauce, wine, and
milk. When we pulled in the next night, weary and cold, there
was a meal waiting.

I saw Bob dispirited only once. He had published yet
another book and was deep into his galvanized research
when he decided to visit his old hometown. I believe he
thought that his old friends would be surprised, maybe awed,
at what had become of Plain Old Bob. They would receive this
decorated war hero, computer expert, and published author
with some degree of respect. Instead, it was more like, "Hi
Bob. You back?" He had done right to leave that sullen and
culturally impoverished small town. He had been mistaken to
have returned.

Bob's Civil War interests extended beyond galvanized men. He published four books: *The Civil War Years: A Day-by-Day Chronicle*; *Civil War Prisons & Escapes*; *The Distaff Civil War*; and *Civil War Medicine – Care and Comfort of the Wounded*.

Bob had quit smoking many years earlier, but it caught up with him. After many unpleasant bouts of radiation and hospital stays he passed away June 22, 2002. August 1, 2002 he was buried at Arlington National Cemetery with full military honors – the caisson, the black horses, the graveside reading, the firing squad, and the playing of Taps. Just before, there had been a memorial service at the Fort Meyers Chapel. I was honored to give the eulogy.

To search further:

http://www.findagrave.com

http://www.arlingtoncemetery.com/redenney.htm

Washington Post, July 21, 2002 MEMORIAM

Grave location: Section 66, Site 6973.

APPENDIX B
GALVANIZED REBELS

———————————

Not all galvanization was Confederate into Union. A small number of Union soldiers, held in Confederate POW camps, joined Confederate fighting units. One of the war's many myths, this one the product of <u>Northern</u> revisionism, is that no Union man ever galvanized into the ranks of the South. At Andersonville itself, five state monuments include "Death before Dishonor," and a 1996 television show, "Andersonville," showed the entire mass of Union soldiers rejecting Captain Wirz's offer of wearing Confederate gray. At Camp Lawton, near Millen, Georgia, four percent of the Union prisoners galvanized. At Florence the estimated galvanization rate was six percent. The subject of galvanized rebels has little appeal to most readers and researchers, the records are often complex and incomplete; obscurity is the clearest result. The following are some of the Confederate units involved.

Galvanized Rebels in the Southeast

Brooks' Battalion, Confederate Regular Infantry (AKA Brooks' Battalion of Foreigners and First Foreign Battalion), commanded by Lt. Col. J. Hampton Brooks, recruited 306 men at the Florence Stockade. The unit was organized in October 1864. Two months later several detachments were sent to Savannah, Georgia, where many deserted and others created serious disturbances. Gen. Hugh Mercer hanged several for mutiny and on December 18 Gen. William Hardee disbanded them and returned the men to Florence with this comment, "Colonel Brooks' battalion . . . was found at Savannah to be utterly untrustworthy. The men deserted in large numbers and finally mutinied . . . The ringleaders were shot." (OR, Ser. II, vol.7, p. 1268.) Their individual records can be found on microfilm in NARA's "Compiled Service Records of Confederate Soldiers Who Served in Organizations Raised Directly by the Confederate Government," reels 72 and 73. There is also a sketch of "Brooks' Foreign Legion" in the South Carolina United Daughters of the Confederacy set, *Recollections and Reflections* (2002), volume XII, pages 538-540.

Tucker's Confederate Regiment (AKA First Foreign Battalion and First Foreign Legion), Lieut. Col. John G. Tucker, commanding, recruited Union soldiers from prisons at Florence, South Carolina, Salisbury, North Carolina, and Richmond, Virginia. Thirty-seven of these men were recruited at the Florence Stockade.

The Eighth Confederate Battalion was organized in December 1864, with 360 men from the Florence Stockade. Originally designated "2nd Foreign Battalion," and later renamed "2nd Foreign Legion," it ended the war under the name of the Eighth Confederate Battalion.

At James Island, South Carolina, the 47th Georgia Infantry took in 150 galvanized rebels, while an unnamed Georgia unit accepted 200 more. (*OR*, 2, 7 {120}, pages 1123-1124.) Two things are clear. First, there can be no doubt that several hundred Union POWs volunteered for Confederate service. Second, an exact clarification of the numbers and named individuals involved awaits some future researcher.

Galvanized Rebels in the Deep South

Today, the village of Egypt, Mississippi, is a crossroads, with a dozen homes and a Baptist church. In 1864, it was the site of a railroad station and a battle.

The Tenth Tennessee Infantry (Confederate) was commanded by Col. John G. O'Neill. He had sent one of his officers, Michael Burke, to recruit Union men held at Millen and Andersonville, Georgia. (Fr. A. H. Ledoux's *The Florence Stockade* shows that he recruited 200 men at Florence.) The men became Burke's Battalion of the Tenth Tennessee. Their new superiors seem to have had some doubts of the true galvanization of these recruits, since they were not issued arms until the night before their first engagement.

What happened next is the subject of some disagreement. The essence is that some of Burke's men quickly surrendered to the Union forces, were embraced by their old adherents, and then served on the western frontier. At Egypt Station they, and the 17th Arkansas, fought two brigades of Brig. Gen. Benjamin Grierson's cavalry. On the night before the fight, six of Burke's men deserted and told the Union forces of the desire of many of the remaining men to make little resistance when attacked. The next day, any story of quick surrender is cast in doubt; Burke's men resisted a charge by the Second New Jersey Cavalry, killing 74 men and 80 horses. The Jersey men did capture more than 500 Confederates, including 253 former Union soldiers, who were shipped to the prison at Alton, Illinois.

The Judge Advocate General's Office in Washington, DC, wanted to try and possibly shoot the 253 rebels. Maj. Gen. Grenville Dodge argued that they would be more useful fighting Indians than being shot. Dodge won. The doubly galvanized men, and 59 genuine former Confederate soldiers, became Companies C and D of the 5th US Volunteers. Their further story is told in Chapter Eight.

Perhaps a thousand Union prisoners volunteered to serve in the Confederate ranks. Their dedication to the Confederate Cause seems to have been tenuous, at best.

APPENDIX C
SOME STATISTICS

Prisons of origin of galvanized Virginians: Point Loo-kout, 169 men. Rock Island, 63 men. Camp Douglas, 56 men. Alton Prison, 5 men. Camp Morton, 4 men.

Virginia galvanized men dying while in service: 27 men, i.e., nine percent.

Virginia galvanized men wounded by Indians: one. Killed by Indians: none.

Virginia galvanized men who deserted: 69, i.e., 24 per-cent, a very high rate of desertion.

Virginia galvanized men who were illiterate: 133, i.e., 46 percent. Illiteracy is defined here as the soldier being un-able to write his own name.

Virginia galvanized men whose records show that they had been vaccinated for smallpox while in Confederate service: 79 men. Not all recruiting centers recorded full med-ical information, so an accurate percentage is not possible.

Twenty-seven galvanized Virginians were discharged for medical reasons before their enlistments were complete: three for diarrhea; three for tuberculosis; and one each for right eye cataract, gonorrhea, syphilis, typhoid, and ulcerated corneas. Seventeen men received medical (usually defined as "disability" or "convalescent") discharges, but with no specific diagnosis visible in their service records.

The system of veteran's pensions became one of the largest factors in American life. Urged on by the Grand Army of the Republic and the Republican Party, the paperwork and the research to identify valid claims became a bureaucracy in itself, with its own huge headquarters, the Pension Building, now the National Building Museum. The Virginia galvanized men were no strangers to this system; 102 applied for a pension. There were 61 applications by widows, usually associated with earlier applications by the husband. There were five applications on behalf of minors and four for mothers. One must note that not every application was approved.

Confederate pensions were established by the various secessionist states, usually long after the war. The methods for researching such are complicated by a very complex system of indexing, a contrast with the fairly straightforward Federal index. In the preparation of this essay on galvanized Virginians the author encountered five men with Confederate pensions: Isaac Jenkins, John Lambert, Gordon Lane, James Patton, and George Taylor.

APPENDIX D
WHAT IS A CMSR?

CMSR stands for Compiled Military Service Record. If a researcher visits the National Archives in Washington, DC, and requests to see the service records of a Union Civil War soldier, he will receive (if the staff hasn't lost or misfiled that record) a stiff paper envelope, about three by seven inches in dimension. Within it, there will be a number of stiff paper cards, each about 2.5 by 6.5 inches. There will be a heading on each card with the soldier's name, rank, company and regiment. Each card covers a two-month period. If the soldier is merely present, there is note saying "Present." Unfortunately, "present" merely means that he was doing what his company was supposed to be doing, but it does not tell what that activity was. If he is away AWOL, or deserted, or sick, or wounded, or detailed to some special assignment, that event will be noted. The first card in each envelope gives mustering-in information, such as age, height, and eye color. The final card gives mustering-out information such as date and place.

The untutored researcher will think he has seen the original records. Not so. Every sixty days, each company of each regiment was required to prepare a muster roll, and transmit it to the War Department. These rolls, roughly 24 by 36 inches, had a note for each soldier in the company. As the pension system mushroomed from hundreds to millions, each application had to be vetted, to verify the soldier's claim of service. The large muster rolls began to deteriorate from frequent handling, with dozens of foldings and unfoldings. Under pressure from veteran's groups, Congress took action. The huge Pension Building was constructed, with desk space for hundreds of copyists. Their work transcribed the muster rolls onto the cards described earlier. The muster rolls were then retired and never again seen by the public. The on-purpose durable cards, filled out with best-quality ink, by staff with good handwriting, are usable still today, and became the basis for analyzing pension claims.

Are these cards accurate? Do they truly reflect the original muster rolls? The now-retired, but still legendary, Michael P. Musick did a study decades ago. He concluded that the CMSRs were highly accurate gleanings from the big original muster rolls.

The "C" in CMSR is truly for "compiled." These cards still exist. They are gradually being filmed and posted on a commercial, subscription website called Fold3. Several large states have yet to be filmed: Pennsylvania and Michigan. The fate of these cards, after filming is complete, is not known. This is an important issue, as demonstrated with the tragedy of the Pension Index.

The Pension Bureau completed an alphabetized card catalog of every one of the millions of applications, with key cataloging numbers, essential to finding the actual pension records. About forty years ago, the National Archives hired a firm to put this index onto film. The contractor did a slipshod job, on 16 mm film, making the images hard to read. They also made all Navy cards, which were on colored card stock, illegible. After this poorly done job was complete, the National Archives destroyed all the original cards. *Res ipsa loquitur.*

Nota bene: Future researchers pursuing such subjects might want to know that there are three indices to the Union Civil War pensions. The first is the alphabetical one described above. The second, most useful to a researcher studying a single regiment, is where the cards are gathered together by state, regiment, and company, with the men arranged alphabetically within each company. The third, rarely used, is chronological by pension number, beginning with pension number one, and ending somewhere beyond one million.

THE INDIAN CAMPAIGN MEDAL

In 1907, War Department General Orders 12 established the Indian Campaign Medal, which is portrayed on the front cover. It was to be awarded for enumerated campaigns or actions against hostile Indians in which United States troops were killed or wounded between 1865 and 1891.

The Federal Code of Regulations described the medal's obverse (front) side as "a mounted Indian facing sinister, wearing a war bonnet, and carrying a spear in his right hand. Above the horseman are the words 'Indian Wars,' and below, on either side of a buffalo skull, the circle is completed by arrowheads, conventionally arranged. On the reverse is a trophy, composed of an eagle perched on a cannon supported by crossed flags, rifles, an Indian shield, spear, quiver of arrows, a Cuban machete, and a Sulu kriss. Below the trophy are the words 'For Service.' The whole is surrounded by a circle composed of the words 'United States Army' in the upper half and thirteen stars in the lower half."

The medal was issued as a one-time decoration only and there were no devices or service stars for those who had participated in multiple actions. The only attachment authorized was a silver citation star, awarded for meritorious or heroic conduct. In the years between 1865 and 1891 only eleven soldiers were awarded this silver star.

To be eligible for the Indian Campaign Medal a soldier had to have service in one of thirteen designated campaigns:

1. Oregon, Idaho, California, Nevada, 1865-1868.
2. Comanches in Kansas, Colorado, Texas, etc., 1867-1875.
3. Modoc War 1872-1873.
4. Arizona Apaches War 1873.
5. Northern Cheyenne and Sioux War 1876-1877.
6. Nez Perce War 1877.
7. Bannock War 1878.
8. Northern Cheyennes War 1878-1879.
9. Sheep-eaters, Piutes, and Bannocks War, summer 1879.
10. Colorado and Utah Utes War, 1879-1880.
11. Arizona and New Mexico Apaches War, 1885-1886.
12. South Dakota Sioux War 1890-1891.
13. Any action in which troops were killed or wounded, 1865-1891.

The author was unable to discover whether any Galvanized Virginians or any of the many other galvanized troops received this decoration, but certainly many seem eligible based on the numerous fatal encounters described in Chapter Eight.

APPENDIX F
COURT-MARTIALED
GALVANIZED YANKEES

During the course of their existence, the United States Volunteers had a total of forty-four general courts-martial. (These records do not include regimental or garrison courts-martial.) The names recorded here are of <u>all</u> court-martialed US Volunteer men, not just Virginians. These findings were generated in the course of ten years of National Archives research conducted by Beverly A. Lowry and the author, and recorded in a Microsoft Access database, under the aegis of The Index Project, Inc., which found and summarized over 75,000 Union courts-martial. This listing of US Volunteer trials may be of use to future researchers.

First regiment: George Brown; Andrew J. Butler; Harry H. Goodrich; William A. Hough; Florence McCarthy (tried twice); and John W. Tyson.

Second regiment: Joseph T. Blankinship; Oram J. Brumley; Patrick Clark; Frank Holmes (tried twice); Thomas Leonard; George W. Mathews; Allen McDonald; John E. Meadows; John Morgan; Henry Pennington; and Julius A. Therrell.

Third regiment: No recorded courts-martial.

Fourth regiment: James H. Carpenter; Marcus L. Clayton; William Gleaton; Walter Glenn; Thomas Kelly; Pearson C. Leady; Thomas Leonard; Michael Mallon; Henry L. Miller; Antonia Mitchell; Jesse Small; Ellis Sones; Lewis W. Spears; and Jacob M. Stover.

Fifth regiment: T. D. Holly; Gragen Jinish; James McCarthy; Henry Peters; Daniel Reynolds; A. C. Sheppard; and S. C. Simmons.

Sixth regiment: Thomas Buchanan; Zachariah Green; Joseph Isaacs; and Patrick Wall.

POSTLUDE

The turn of the millennium has brought a torrent of lost friends, most of them carried across the Great Divide, with a few still lingering in their corporeal bodies, but having lost the cognition that made them so wonderful. They were all friends who were mentors, co-workers, healers, encouragers, or just warm companions on the journey of life. Here of some of those whom I cherished so much and miss so deeply.

Bill Brown, PhD; Bob Collins, BA; Charles Cress, MD; Bill Dickerson, MD; Mary Ann Gossett, LVN; Richard Hudgens, MD; Ron Hughes, MFA; Wolfgang Lederer, MD; Jim Mickle, MD; Ed Milligan, LT COL USA RETD; Buzz Mills, BA; Mike Neal, MD; Leonard Nuckolls, BA; Donald Poulton, DDS; Sidney Raffel, MD; J. M. Stubblebine, MD; Budge Weidman, BA; and Jack Welsh, MD.

With rue my heart is laden, for golden friends I had,
For many a rose-lipped maiden, and many a lightfoot lad.

By brooks too broad for leaping, the lightfoot boys are laid;
The rose-lipt girls are sleeping, in fields where roses fade.

A. E. Housman

INDEX

Virginia Confederate Regiments

Errors, Omissions, Additions, and *Hintertreppenwitze*

An additional four men are added to the roster, thanks to Michel P. Musick and his deeply researched *Sixth Virginia Cavalry*.

Conrad Bodencamp was born Feb. 1, 1843 in Hamburg. Enlisted April 5, 1862 in Co. G as "Henry E. West," a substitute. He was previously a Sgt. in Co. D, 1st S.C. Arty., from which he had deserted while on furlough. He was captured at Snickers Gap July 17, 1863 and confined at Point Lookout. There he was able to sign his own name, had been vaccinated, and had suffered with chronic diarrhea in 1863. He was in Co. B, 1st US Volunteers, where he was acting QM Sgt. in May 1864, and in July 1864 promoted to Drum Major. In October

1865 he was on detached service. He mustered out November 27, 1865 at Fort Leavenworth. He did not apply for a pension.

James K. Clearwater was born in Orange, N.Y. Confederate records are lost. He was captured June 5, 1864 at Cold Harbor, and confined at Point Lookout, where he was noted to be a 21-year old baker, able to write his own name. He had had scarlet fever in 1859 and had been vaccinated. He enlisted in Co. K, 1st US volunteers, served two months, then deserted in New York City, taking all his Union equipment. He did not apply for a pension.

Reubin J. Murray (Reuben Murry) was born in Fauquier Co. He enlisted April 24, 1861 in Co. H. He was AWOL nine days in January 1862. In May 1862 he was detailed as a courier at Madison CH. He was AWOL again in August 1863. He deserted in Fauquier Co. in December 1863 and was captured. At Point Lookout he enlisted in Co. G, 1st US Volunteers and served until May 21, 1866 when he was mustered out at Fort Leavenworth. His CMSR contains a single page. After the war he farmed at Springvale, Fairfax Co. He died in April 1904. He made no pension application.

Joseph Gustavus Weaver was born in Rappahannock Co. He enlisted in Co. B January 1, 1863. He deserted eleven months later and was captured December 6, 1863 at Culpeper CH. He wrote from Point Lookout, "I am a Union man and always was." He enlisted October 12, 1864 in Co. D, 4th US Volunteers, where he was noted to be a 19-year old carpenter, 5'6", with black eyes and able to write his own name. In October 1864 he was promoted to corporal. He deserted May

8, 1865 at Cincinnati. After the war he lived in Boston and Scrabble, both in Virginia's Culpeper County, and received a Virginia pension. Died 1937 at the age of 97 and is buried in Old Joe Weaver Cemetery, Boston, Va.

Veteran's pensions, north and south, were issued subject to various restrictions. Deserters, those who switched sides, and soldiers known to have "vicious and immoral habits" were not to receive pensions or benefits such as life in a veteran's home. Among the Virginia galvanized men, twenty-one seem to have received Union benefits (or at least, forgiveness) in spite of these guidelines. They are clustered here and summarized, in alphabetical order, for any future researcher studying the pension issue.

Samuel A. Anderson deserted in 1865 and received an honorable discharge in 1925. John T. Bray deserted in 1864 and applied for a Union pension in 1901. Horace Brown deserted in 1863 and applied for a Union disability pension in 1872. Thomas W. Byrd deserted in 1865 taking $140 in government stores. The charges were dropped. James A. Conner deserted in 1865, taking $156 in government property. He was returned to duty without trial. The charges were dropped in 1888, after which he received a pension. When he died in 1925 his widow applied to keep receiving benefits. Samuel T. DeLong deserted in 1865. The charges were dropped in 1891. Jacob Heater enlisted in the 1st US Volunteers and deserted. Later he was given the privilege of living in the Confederate Soldiers Home in Richmond, after having deserted from both armies. James McPeak deserted in 1865. Charges were dropped in 1885. In 1916 he requested a copy of his Union discharge. James P. Neikirk deserted in 1865 and received an honorable discharge in 1888. James M. Oslin served nearly all his time in Union hospitals, doing no real duty. He received a disability pension in 1888, which continued for his widow in 1908.

Matthew M. Petty deserted in 1865. In 1885 the charges were dropped, followed promptly by a pension application. William E. Quigley deserted in 1865. In 1925 the charges were dropped. A few weeks later he applied for a pension, which was denied. Marion Quillin deserted in 1865. In 1885 the charges were dropped and he was granted a discharge. In 1932 the family applied for a free Federal gravestone. Leonard Schools deserted in 1865. In 1925 the charges were dropped and he was issued a discharge. George W. Stogdall was discharged in 1865 as too sick from gonorrhea to serve as a soldier. In 1895 he received a disability pension. In 1910 the government continued payments to his wife. William Sweeney deserted in 1865. In 1913 he requested an honorable discharge, which was granted. Soon after, he began collecting a Federal disability pension, which continued to his widow in 1922. Samuel Thompson deserted twice and threatened to kill his officers. In 1890 he applied for a disability pension. John W. Tyson deserted in 1865. In 1889 the charges were dropped and he was issued a discharge. The following year he began receiving a disability pension. These benefits passed onto his widow in 1912. John Wilson deserted in 1865, taking $100 in QM stores. In 1895, he applied for a disability pension.

Each Confederate state had its own pension system for war veterans. The first Virginia pensions were issued in 1888, aimed specifically at the physically disabled who were also in poverty. There were no "loyalty" restrictions, probably because no one imagined that a legless or armless veteran would somehow be faking his needs. The issue of who "deserved" what seems to have arisen, and the Act of 1900 contained a clause, in paragraph two, that the applicant must have been a "true and loyal soldier." This would seem to exclude those who had "galvanized."

Two years later, the restrictions became more specific. The applicant, by signing, was certifying "that during the war I was loyal and true to my duty, and never at any time, deserted my command or voluntarily abandoned my post of duty," words that seem to further close the doors to galvanized men. Further, the Act of 1902 required the signatures of a number of witnesses. The forms to be attached to the application called for affidavits in nine different categories: Oath of Resident Witnesses; Affidavit of Comrades; Affidavit of Witnesses, not Comrades; Certificate of Physician; Certificate of Camp of Confederate Veterans; Certificate of Ex-Confederate Soldiers; Certificate of Commissioner of Revenue; Certificate of Pension Board; and Certificate of Judge. The direct witnesses were cautioned that they are confirming that the veteran was "true and loyal." Serious effort was made to assure that the veteran was indeed a veteran and could confirm his regiment and commanding officer. (Robert E. L. Krick was most helpful on these points.)

The roster in Chapter Ten contains five galvanized men who seem to have received Virginia pensions. In addition, there is J G. Weaver from Musick's *6th Virginia Cavalry*. Further research in additional original records has clarified their stories.

A note on Confederate sources. The vast jumble of Confederate soldier papers was organized onto CMSR cards by the War Records Office, somewhere around 1900-1920, before the National Archives existed. The microfilming of the Confederate CMSRs was funded in the 1930s by a wealthy South Carolina woman. Neither of these labor-intensive projects would be possible today. The Virginia pension applications have recently been digitized by the Library of Virginia and are available on the Internet. Though some are pixilated, the majority are quite useful.

Isaac C. Jenkins enlisted in Company L, 10th Virginia Infantry, at Camp Johnson, on August 12, 1861. He then went AWOL from October 12, 1861 to January 1, 1862. His CMSR says he deserted April 6, 1862. However, he was present at the Battle of Chancellorsville where says he was wounded in the right temple. He was admitted to Chimborazo Hospital May 12, 1863 with a diagnosis of Vulnus Sclopeticum (gunshot wound). He deserted twelve days later. Federal records say he was captured at Bermuda Hundred in May 1864. At Point Lookout he was noted to be age 20, 5' 7", with blue eyes and unable to write his own name. He enlisted in Company E, 2nd US Volunteers at Point Lookout on October 21, 1864, and was stationed in Norfolk, Virginia, where he was confined for some malfeasance. There, in February 1865, he deserted from the Union army and was never caught. In the years between the war and 1880, he married one Elizabeth and sired six children. In April 1888, he put his mark of "X" on a Virginia pension application, swearing that because of his Chancellorsville wound "he can do no work which requires standing, cannot perform more than one-third manual labor than he could do before." In an undated letter in the file attesting that since the wound he has been "so seriously and permanently disabled as to be afterwards incapacitated for said service until the close of the said war—and that he is now and has been since said wound prevented during a great part of his time from performing manual labor." In his formal application for aid for being "maimed or disabled in the war between the States," dated April 2, 1888, he listed "...by a Minié ball wound in the right temple. (He is now age forty-three.) He signed with an "X" on April 2, 1888, having not gained the ability to write even his own name.

On the 24th of April, 1888, a judge of the Page County court certified that he is "fully satisfied from the evidence adduced before me that each and all of the facts set forth in the within application are true; that the applicant is the identical person named in the application; that the application is for these reasons approved, and is therefore certified that Isaac C. Jenkins is entitled to receive annually from the State of Virginia the sum of Fifteen dollars."

There is one more slip of paper in his Virginia file, dated June 18, 1887. (Here he is apparently being paid the year <u>before</u> his pension application.) "Luray, Va. Received of Auditor of Public Accounts, check No. 9256 on Planters Natl. Bank for $60; the same being payment in full of the commutation money allowed me by an Act of the General Assembly of Virginia of 1885-6, making an appropriation to maimed and disabled soldiers and marines." The slip is signed by Jenkins' attorney.

Isaac is buried in plot 20#81 of the cemetery of Western State Hospital, Staunton, Virginia.

Should one be skeptical of the merit of Jenkins' claim, a man who deserted each army at least once, was jailed at least once, was able to serve two more years in spite a "disabling" head wound, and was able to farm and sire six children over a twenty year period? On the other hand, if he was truly disabled, how could a family of eight survive on fifteen dollars a year? The pathos and puzzles of the Civil War live on.

John W. Lambert. Five men with the name of John W. Lambert served in Virginia forces. One John W. Lambert was in Co. B, 25th Va. Cavalry. He was from Lee County and was off sick at home most of 1864. He was receiving a Va. pension in 1920. He was not a galvanized Virginian. A second John W. Lambert was in the 62nd Mounted Va. Infantry. He enlisted in Pendleton County, (West) Va. and was present on duty as of September 1863. He, too, was not a galvanizer.

A third John W. Lambert was from central Va. and served in the 21st Va. Infantry. He disappears from the CSA records in October 1862. Again, not our man. The next candidate, a resident of Brunswick Co., enlisted in August 1864 in the 14th Va. Infantry and was taken prisoner en route to Appomattox.

He, too, is no galvanizer. Which brings us to John W. Lambert, who enlisted in Co. C, 22nd Va. Cavalry, in Tazewell Co., October 31, 1863. He was taken prisoner at Fisher's Hill August 22, 1864. He was sent to Point Lookout, where he enlisted in Co. D, 4th US Volunteers. He is clearly the galvanized Lambert. Federal CMSR records show he enlisted at Point Lookout October 12, 1864 and had been born in "Tazzel, Va." He was absent sick at General Hospital, Fort Sully, June 22, 1865. In September he was transferred to Sioux City, where he died the following month of typhoid fever.

Did he receive a pension from either side? The Union records clearly show his mother, on October 15, 1892 applying for a pension. Was their a Virginia application? The records indicate one from the Lambert of the 25th Va. Infantry, none from the galvanized Lambert.

Gordon Hall Lane enlisted for one year in Co. C, 54th Va. Infantry September 10, 1861, at Christiansburg. He was captured July 3, 1864 at Mt. Zion Church, near Marietta, Ga. He was held first at Nashville, then forwarded to the military prison at Louisville. From Louisville he went to Camp Douglas, near Chicago. There he enlisted in Co. K, 6th US Volunteers. His service there is documented in the Roster. In his twenty pages of Federal pension application, there are numerous bits of information. Most of his life he lived at "Vicar Switch," which now appears as Vicker Switch, a hamlet southwest of Blacksburg. His parents were Allen Lane and Indiana Bell. On September 17, 1867, Gordon and Mary J. Williams were joined in marriage by the Rev. C. A. Miller, a Methodist minister. He was 22; she was 18. They had seven children: Lucy (1868); William (1870); Robert (1872); John (1878); Walter (1882); James (1884); and Earnest (1891).

In 1872, he applied for a Federal pension, citing "rheumatism from winter exposure at Fort Cottonwood." The claim was rejected: "Disability not sufficient." He applied again in 1907. The pension board requested his Confederate service. An entry notes that he was "not a conscript," i.e., he had voluntarily entered Confederate service, which counted against him, but the ultimate reason for his second and final rejection was that he had enlisted in Union service after January 1, 1865. He died at 9:30 AM, February 16, 1914, of "myocardial degeneration," and was buried at Mt. Calvary Cemetery. His physician was Dr. A. M. Showalter. In October 1917, his widow applied for a pension. She was awarded $25 a month, increased to $40 a month in 1928. Her date of death not noted.

On May 7, 1910, a Gordon Lane of Montgomery Co., Va., a former member of the 54th Va. Infantry, applied for a Virginia pension. In response to Question 10 of the application, "When and why did you leave the service," he replied, "I was captured 1863 or 1864 and was kept in prison 10 months." He does not mention his Federal service. Occupation? "Farming and other light employment." He added, "My disability partially originates from service while in the (Confederate) army." He gave as the names of comrades who has served with him, John M. Hudgins and John F. Woods, both of Rogers, a small town a mile south of Christiansburg. Confederate CMSRs show a John M. Hudgins and a John F. Wood, both of Co. C and both enlisted at Christiansburg. On the next page they appear on sworn affidavits. There is also a "Certificate of Physician." On May 9, 1910, H. F. Lushbaugh, MD, wrote "Rheumatism and disability on account of age. Therefore the applicant is partially deprived of ability to perform his usual and customary occupation or any other occupation for a livelihood." (The Hambrecht database shows Harmon Franklin Lushbaugh, born in 1848 in Virginia, 1871 graduate of Washington University School of Medicine, Baltimore, Md., and practicing medicine after 1900 in Montgomery Co. Va.

From the records available, it would seem that during the period 1910 through 1914 Gordon Lane received veteran's benefits from the Commonwealth of Virginia.

George W. Taylor (the "W" is probably Washington) represents a particular challenge. Three men of that name were galvanized and served in Co. K, 5th US Volunteers; Co. F, 1st US Volunteers; and Co. G, 2nd US Volunteers. None appear to have filed for a Union pension.

Confederate service is a greater challenge. There were thirty-one George W. Taylors and seven G. W. Taylors in Virginia service. One such served in Co. A, 5th Va. Infantry and later rode with Mosby, long enough that later in the war the Union put a price on his head. He applied for a Virginia pension in 1916. A George W. Taylor served in Co. F, 1st Battalion, Richmond Local Defense Troops, and is buried in Shockoe Hill Cemetery, Richmond. He seems an unlikely prospect. Even less likely was George W. Taylor buried in Virginia's Hampton National Cemetery. He was in the 8th Pennsylvania Cavalry. A George W. Taylor served in the 55th Va. Infantry. He went missing in action in April 1863, but there is nothing to link him to the US Volunteers. A George W. Taylor of Co. A, 23rd Va. Inf. was wounded at Chancellorsville and received a $15 pension under the 1888 law, but again no known history of galvanization. A George W. Taylor of the Powhatan Light Artillery died in 1912, and is buried in Richmond's Hollywood Cemetery, but again no discernible link to the galvanized men.

In brief, there seems to be no George W. Taylor in the Union pension records, and only two discovered in the Virginia pension records and they cannot be shown to have served in the US Volunteers.

James Patton (Patten) has a few mysteries. James Russell Patton (1841-1919) served in Co. A, 63rd Va. Inf. He deserted July 4, 1862, but returned. He was AWOL 9 months in 1863 and 2 months in 1864. He was taken prisoner May 20, 1864 at Calhoun, Ga. and sent to Rock Island Prison, where he enlisted in Co. K, 2nd US Volunteers. He applied for a Union invalid pension in April 1883. In February 1914 his widow applied for his pension. She died at Speedwell, Va. (a tiny hamlet in Wythe Co.) January 6, 1919. They are buried in the Speedwell Methodist Cemetery.

James Robert Patton (1847-1908) served in Co. F, 45th Va. Inf. He was sick in September 1861 and again in June 1862, this time at Giles C.H. He was still on the rolls in the fourth quarter of 1864. He has no Union service record and is buried in the Mechanicsburg Cemetery, Bland, Va. The Virginia pension application was by James Houston Patton, a civil engineer who had worked, pre-war, for the US Coast Survey, and enlisted in Co. H, 1st Va. Inf. (Williams Rifles).

Joseph Gustavus Weaver filed for a Virginia pension on September 9, 1922. He stated, "I was taken prisoner 1863 and was held in prison at Point Lookout until the Surrender." He omitted his service in the 4th US Volunteers and his professing that he was "always a Union man"

In brief, it would appear that three men who served in Union galvanized regiments later received Virginia pensions.

Idle
Winter
Press

Made in the USA
San Bernardino, CA
11 May 2016